JUNGLE DAYS

JUNGLE DAYS

BEING THE EXPERIENCES OF AN AMERICAN WOMAN DOCTOR IN INDIA

ARLEY MUNSON, M.D.

GYAN

Published by

GYAN

Gyan Publishing House
5, Ansari Road
Daryaganj, New Delhi-110002
Phone: 011-47034999, 9811692060
E-mail: books@gyanbooks.com

Distribution Network
gyanbooks.com
India, USA, Canada, UK, Australia, France

ISBN : 978-81-212-9540-6 (PB)
First Published, 1913

2nd Impression 2023

Printed at: Gyan Press, Delhi.

JUNGLE DAYS
Author: ARLEY MUNSON, M.D.

Dr. Arley Munson

JUNGLE DAYS

BEING THE EXPERIENCES OF AN AMERICAN WOMAN DOCTOR IN INDIA

BY

ARLEY MUNSON, M.D.

ILLUSTRATED

1913

TO MY MOTHER

FOREWORD

When my friends ask me: "Why did you leave the splendid opportunities of your own country for the discomforts and dangers of a far-off pagan land?" I feel inclined to make the submissive reply heard so frequently from the lips of the meek-voiced women of India: *"Kismet! Adrushtam!* It was my destiny. How else should I find peace?"

It was during my early childhood that, on turning the leaves of a mission book, I found an illustration representing a Hindu mother throwing her baby into the gaping jaws of a crocodile, as a sacrifice to the gods; and I asked my mother what the dreadful picture meant. When she had explained it to me, I hid my tearful face on her shoulder, and, my heart swelling with sorrow and pity, I resolved to "hurry and grow up" that I might go out to India and "save those poor little babies."

In the years that followed I learned the tragedy of the Indian woman's existence, and the smoldering resolve of my childhood flamed into a mature and steady determination to spend a part of my life practicing medicine and surgery in India, with the hope that by healing the body I might reach the mind and heart and lead them, if ever so short a distance, out of the darkness of ignorance and vice that surrounded them.

My medical college and hospital studies completed, I left New York for India.

On my journey to India and during the five years of my life there I kept a fairly accurate record of my experiences, from which record the present book is largely taken.

The illustrations are from photographs of the actual persons and places mentioned in my story. I avail myself of this opportunity to thank Rev. Charles W. Posnett of Medak, India, for his cordial and generous permission to use the photographs taken in his district.

I have touched but lightly on the evangelical side of mission life. My effort to rid my patients of physical ailments occupied my time so fully that I was obliged to resign their spiritual guidance to my thoroughly able and willing colleagues.

This book, then, apart from rough sketches of scenes as they came before me in my travels from Bombay to Calcutta, from Kashmir to Tuticorin, is simply a glimpse into warmly beating human hearts hidden away in the depths of Indian jungle-villages, where their "Doctor Mem Sahib" found them, loved them, and tried, in her imperfect, human way, to help them.

Though at times the thunders of defeat and tragedy almost deafened me, rang always high above the tumult the clear, sweet note of that happiness promised in Mr. Kipling's vision of the future, when "... no one shall work for money, and no one shall work for fame, But each for the joy of the working ..."

CONTENTS

CHAPTER		PAGE
I.	Bombay	1
II.	Life at Sholapur	6
III.	Wayside Sketches	18
IV.	The City of Palaces	22
V.	Benares	25
VI.	Agra	27
VII.	Sholapur Again	31
VIII.	Hyderabad	33
IX.	My Indian Home	37
X.	The Rains	46
XI.	Our Indian Friends	51
XII.	American Thanksgiving Day in India	59
XIII.	Christmas	80
XIV.	Dream Days Among the Himalayas	82
XV.	Back to the Plains	85
XVI.	We Go A-Touring	91
XVII.	On Horseback and Off	103
XVIII.	The Jahtra	111
XIX.	Rice Christians	116
XX.	God's Out-of-Doors	121
XXI.	Off to Kashmir	133
XXII.	Summer Sightseeing	142
XXIII.	Women of India	153
XXIV.	Jungle Foes	168
XXV.	New Camping Grounds	173
XXVI.	Mahorrum	188
XXVII.	An April Holiday	195
XXVIII.	Swadeshi	200

CONTENTS

CHAPTER		PAGE
XXIX.	To the Hills Away	209
XXX.	Darjiling	216
XXXI.	Hospital Lights and Shades	224
XXXII.	Young Hopefuls	248
XXXIII.	Penetrating the Wilds	255
XXXIV.	Fantastic Summer's Heat	267
XXXV.	Strenuous Times	271
XXXVI.	The Cholera Terror	285
XXXVII.	Farewells	295

LIST OF ILLUSTRATIONS

FACING PAGE

Dr. Arley Munson . . . . *Frontispiece*
Medak Dispensary, vaccination day 42
Indian carpenters at work 60
String bed of India, the common sleeping cot . . . 60
In the Medak Dispensary 70
Mahomedan Madas bringing gratitude offering of sheep garlanded with flowers 70
Dr. Munson operating in Medak Hospital 76
Corner of medical ward, Medak Hospital 76
Dora Chatterjee 86
Toddy-drawing 124
Swing bridge of Kashmir 134
Snake charmers and jugglers 134
Kashmiri women 138
Watering the rice-fields 182
Tree ferns in India 212
Medak Zevana Hospital, prayer corner, surgical ward 226
A country cart stopping at Medak Hospital . . . 232
Medak touring outfit 232
Boys' playground, Medak 250
Girls' playground, Medak 250
Medak doctor on tour 256
Medak nurse visiting the sick in a palanquin . . . 256
Sunday Bible Class, Medak 292

JUNGLE DAYS

I

BOMBAY

BOMBAY to-morrow morning!" exclaimed the captain cheerily as we rose from dinner, and we knew our long voyage was ended. Ocean life and ocean friendships had been delightful, but that last evening, instead of the usual merry gathering on deck, everybody, busy with his own thoughts, was strangely quiet.

At midnight I still gazed out over the water, the vast loneliness of the sea sinking into my soul. My dream of work in India would soon be reality. For years I had heard my little sisters of India calling to me to help them, and now I was nearly there. The thought almost overwhelmed me, for who was I that I should presume to teach others how to live! Deep down in my heart, I longed—Oh, so desperately!—to turn traitor to my ideals and go back home. But this was cowardly indeed; so, stifling a sigh which was half a sob, I strengthened myself with a whispered, "No more backward glances! Eastward ho!" and went to my stateroom, where I had a comforting good-night chat with Sonubai.

Sonubai was one of my college mates who was traveling with me on her way home to Sholapur. In response to the cordial invitation of her parents, Dr. and Mrs. Keskar (those Brahmans converted to Christianity who did such noble, self-sacrificing work among the sufferers in the recent terrible famines and who later became the medical superintendents of a Christian orphanage and leper asylum at Sholapur), I had decided to make my home with them until my plans for work should mature.

When we rose next morning everybody was in a fever of excitement, for there before us, a horseshoe of purest sapphire blue, lay the harbor of Bombay.

My eyes eagerly scanned every detail: stately steamships and other ocean-going craft lay well out from the land; *tom-tits,* curious little sailboats manned by native boatmen, darted here and there; and the white shore and green trees afforded a soothing background to the gaudy display of color on the pier, where hundreds of the Indian men of Bombay in gala raiment—a few foreigners and white-clad Englishmen among them—had come to welcome our giant ship from over-seas.

We had left the ship for the tender and were approaching the pier when Sonubai exclaimed delightedly, "There's Father!" and in another moment Dr. Keskar and Rev. Dr. Karmarkar, an Indian Christian of Bombay, were heartily greeting us. The customs ordeal ended, we drove toward Dr. Karmarkar's home.

With slow tread and downcast face, women in draperies of every hue and texture passed through the streets, their jewels almost covering face, neck, arms, and legs, and jingling at every step. A few of the men were quietly dressed, but many would have put a peacock to shame, as, in blue coat, magenta waistcoat, red trousers, rose-pink turban, and yellow shoes, or in some other color scheme quite as varied, they shuffled along. The whining cry of blind beggars in simple loin-cloth pierced the babel that surrounded us. And there were the babies of the city, carried on their mothers' hips or running about the streets, their shiny brown skin alone clothing their chubby bodies.

Occasionally an English soldier or civilian in khaki or white duck passed through the crowds, his trim costume and ruddy Western face strangely at variance with the life about him.

From the din of the crowded, unsavory bazaar, with its fat shopkeepers, its tiny, open shops, and the dusty confusion of its wares, we were glad to come into the wide, green Esplanade Road. Here the passing throngs were like a story-book pageant: English ladies and gentlemen in summer habit galloped by on spirited horses, or, exquisitely dressed in Hyde Park or Fifth Avenue style, drove leisurely along in open carriages; military officers in uniform rode recklessly; a palanquin, closely curtained and containing some "pride-of-the-harem," was borne past, the women servants following on horseback and an Indian gentleman—husband or son—cantering by the side of the palanquin, each hand holding a rein and the arms flopping negligently; and dark-skinned *ayahs* in snowy muslins were there, in charge of daintily dressed English children.

At the Karmarkar house, Mrs. Karmarkar, who had taken her medical degree from the same college in Philadelphia from which I was graduated, met us with warm hospitality, and in the evening she and Dr. Karmarkar gave a feast—*jawan*—to all the friends who had arrived that day in India.

The floor was prettily decorated with a design in red chalk, while exquisite red roses formed the centerpiece. In full evening dress, we sat about, Turk-fashion, on bright-colored rugs, and ate with our fingers from the banana leaves on which the food was served, while garlands of pink roses and white jasmine around our necks added gaiety to the jolly, informal feast. The gentleman who sat beside me taught me the table etiquette of the Hindu. Food should be eaten with the right hand, only the thumb and the first two fingers—even those not below the first joint—coming in contact with the food; water should be poured from the glass into the mouth without touching the lips. That finger and glass affair may sound easy. Try it! Although I enjoyed the Indian food, the meal seemed like the old picnic meals of childhood, more sweet and spicy things than things substantial.

With teas, dinners, receptions, and services at the various mission institutions, the American missionaries and Dr. Keskar's friends among the Indian Christians filled our time so pleasantly that it seemed but a turn of the kaleidoscope before our Bombay visit came to an end and we were off for Sholapur.

II

LIFE AT SHOLAPUR

ALL the way to Sholapur, Sonubai and I had our railway coach to ourselves. Along each side of the roomy compartment ran an eight-foot, leather-cushioned seat, and above each of these seats hung a wide shelf, also leather-cushioned, constituting an "upper berth," which could be hooked back against the wall when not in use. As there was floor space enough between the lower seats and the tiny but complete dressing-room to accommodate all our trunks and bundles, we had the coolies place our baggage inside our own coach. Then, wrapping our rugs about us, we stretched ourselves comfortably on the long seats and slept soundly till the train rolled into Sholapur.

At their Orphanage on the outskirts of Sholapur, where, because of the plague in the city, the Keskars were camping, we were met by the children of the institution, hundreds of barefooted, brown-faced boys and girls, the boys in turban, *dhoti* (draped trousers) and coat of spotless white, the girls with their graceful red *sari* flung loosely over head and shoulders and falling in long pleats to the ground. As we approached, they burst into a song of joyous greeting—the poor lepers joining in from the distance. When, with bright smiles of welcome and a lusty, "Salaam!" the children had finished the song, and Sonubai's mother and two younger sisters had greeted her with tearful embraces and me with courteous warmth, there began one of the strangest, most bewitching dances I had ever seen. A company of about twenty small boys divided into two lines. With body and limbs moving in perfect rhythm to the sound of their crude castanets and to the loud beating of a drum, they stood first on one foot, then on the other; whirled round and round; wound in and out of the opposite line in a graceful series of intertwinings; sank to a sitting posture on their heels; then rose again light as air. All this again and again, slowly at first, then faster and faster, until the little dancers, exhausted, dropped laughing to the ground amid our loud applause.

As we passed along, group after group came toward us, their leader throwing garlands of pink roses and yellow marigolds over our heads, until we reached the cool, roofed veranda where we listened to a speech of welcome from Dr. Keskar, followed by prayers and hymns of gratitude for our safe arrival.

Although I did not understand the vernacular, I could easily read in the faces of the little ones gathered about me happiness and comfort and a sincere love for "Papa" and "Mamma," as they call Dr. and Mrs. Keskar. It was hard to realize that many of the chubby, happy-faced boys and girls gathered about me were the famine children of 1899 and 1900, the pathetic little skeletons which the press throughout the world so vividly described and photographed.

The greeting ceremonies ended, I was introduced to Indian home life.

With unlimited hospitality, the Keskar family did all they could to give me pleasure, Mrs. Keskar personally superintending the preparation of English food for me—the Indian curries, hot with chilis, were painful to my throat—while Guramma, the cook, deftly turned it out from pots and pans in use on the mud stove. There are no chimneys in Indian village houses, but Guramma, laughing and chatting happily over her work, seemed not at all inconvenienced by the clouds of smoke rolling over her head and filling the kitchen, though I could not even pass through the room without a violent fit of coughing.

LIFE AT SHOLAPUR

My day began with Suernamala. That impressive name belonged to my small handmaiden who, from morning till night, except during school hours, was somewhere close at hand. When the morning sun roused me from sleep I could see Suernamala's plump figure flitting about the room. Observing that I was awake, she would bow low in a respectful *salaam,* and summon Bhagu, her assistant (India is a land of assistant unto assistant), to help her bring my *chota hazrai* (little breakfast), a simple meal of tea and toast and jelly. Frequently, when the child was grateful to me for some trifling favor, she would stoop and kiss the hem of my gown. I tried in vain to break her of this habit, but, in spite of all my explanations, she would tearfully implore me not to consider her unworthy to touch even my clothing, so I submitted with what grace I might.

Most of the day was spent in attending to the various ailments of the children, for, soon after coming to Sholapur, Sonubai and I had started a little dispensary for the Orphanage.

Then, as twilight came on, we would stroll about the compound, feeling like the "Pied Piper of Hamelin," for children surrounded us on every side and followed in a long stream behind, clinging to our dresses and fingertips, and chattering merrily to each other and to us.

At night, after the children slept, Sonubai and I would sit in low chairs by the little mother's side and listen while she sang to us the sweet Marathi hymns or narrated, with a pretty mixture of English and Marathi, the old legends of Hindu mythology.

In the midst of this peaceful existence would come the startling sights and sounds of the jungle, so that for days I was surprised at nothing but the lack of a surprise. Now the cry of "*Sahp!*" would ring through the air; some one had seen a snake, and the schoolboys would arm themselves with heavy sticks and seek out the reptile—cobra or python—which had little chance to escape. Again, some one would shout that a mad dog was in the compound—the life of the pariah dog, the homeless, pitiful scavenger of the Orient, frequently ends in hydrophobia—and a moment later the shrieks of the beast as he was clubbed to death would send shivers down my spine. Milder surprises were the howls of the jackal, filling the night with wild, weird sound; a fox dashing through the compound; an owl flying into the house; or a stately camel stalking slowly along the dusty road, a dark-faced, wild-looking man of the desert on its back.

As a drove of camels passed one day Dr. Keskar persuaded the driver to give me a ride. The camel, not half so pleased as I, grumbled most disagreeably while he knelt for the mount. The great pack on his back was covered with one of our own rugs, the creature emitted more of those hideous grunts, and then I held for life to the pack-ropes while he slowly rose to his feet. When the camel knew that his driver was determined I should have a ride, he took to me more kindly; so, doing my best to balance myself and to sway with the dreadful sweeping swing of that great hump, I rode with more triumph than dignity all around the compound.

When Christmas came—my first Christmas in the tropics—it seemed to me that I was living in a dream. The weather was perfect, the sky, an intense, dazzling blue, the clouds mere flecks of down, and tiny zephyrs, fragrant with the breath of roses and lemon-grass, caressed my cheek with the soft touch of a baby's hand. Friendly sparrows hopped about the floor or chirped overhead among the rafters; lizards scuttled along the wall in the sunshine; tiny squirrels frisked about the doorstep, or, half shyly, half impudently, peeped in at us. From the windows we could see a round Eastern well with a green orchard in the background. Little brown boys frolicked under the trees or splashed with delight in the pond; goats with their kids hopped among the rocks or, standing on their hind legs, reached eager mouths to the young leaves above them; emerald green parrakeets skimmed through the air; and the cooing of the jungle doves mingled with the raucous cawing of a flock of crows in a neighboring tree.

During Christmas Eve, and all through the night, groups of men and boys had come beneath our windows singing Christmas carols in the good, old-fashioned way; and now on Christmas Day, the compound resounded with the song and laughter of the children at their games; even the poor lepers seemed full of Christmas spirit; and life was good to live.

The coming of the bangle-man added to the pleasure and excitement. Under Mrs. Keskar's directions, he gave a pair of the bright-colored glass trinkets to each of the schoolgirls, the vain little creatures insisting on the tiniest bangles in spite of the pain which brought the tears to their eyes as the bangle-man coaxed the bangles over their hands. As a guest of the house, I also was decorated. I refused to be tortured, however, and, greatly to the bangle-man's disgust, insisted on a fair-sized pair of bangles which slipped easily over my hands.

After the distribution of gifts to the children

of the Orphanage, the Keskar family and I went to the Leper Asylum. Although in a few of the poor, doomed lepers no outward sign of the dread disease could be detected, most of them had the bleared eyes, and seamed, swollen features of advanced leprosy, and many had neither fingers nor toes.

For the time being they had lost the hopeless look which, sooner or later, comes into the eyes of lepers, and delightedly they grasped the treasures held out to them, responding with a loud "Tankoo!" and a graceful *salaam*. Three-year-old Rubi did her best, but could only wave her hand in an uncertain way and piece out the gesture with a dimpling smile. I shuddered to think of the wretched fate of that bright babe. Even then she showed the telltale spots!

The presents given, the lepers sang their native songs for us with drum and castanet accompaniment, and then we returned to the Orphanage and the Christmas dinner.

Poolau (rice and goat-meat boiled together) takes the place of our turkey at home, and the children's eyes glistened as, seated on the ground in perfect content, they dipped their fingers again and again into the heaped-up plates, or drank long draughts of water from their tin cups.

Baby Assiabai was too young for the *poolau*,

but her coos and gurgles showed that she also enjoyed her Christmas. Baby Assiabai represents one of Dr. Keskar's medical triumphs. A few months before Christmas, Dr. Keskar found her, a tiny babe on the very verge of starvation, in a corner of a village hut. Lean, hungry-eyed rats gnawed greedily at her fingers and toes, and, close by, five dead bodies, plague-stricken, lay huddled. The doctor brought the wailing child to his Orphanage and put her in charge of a foster-mother who tenderly nursed her back to life. The wounds of the hands and feet soon healed, the wasted form rounded out, and dimples played in the plump cheeks as she laughed at our attempts to amuse her.

Our one sadness of the Christmas-time was to find that Kanku had the leprosy. Kanku, a child of South India and a stranger indeed among our Marathis, often wept bitterly over the thoughtless teasing of the other children about her South country language and customs; the only happiness of her timid, home-loving Indian heart was to stand outside the lepers' inclosure and talk with two or three leper girls who were from her own district in the South. Then, on Christmas Day, we found in Kanku unmistakable signs of leprosy and gently told her so with a shrinking dread of her misery at the bitter truth. To our surprise, Kanku laughed joyfully, "Now I can be with my own people," and rushed away to her little countrywomen in the Lepers' Asylum.

New Year's Day was celebrated by dining with a prominent Brahman family of Sholapur. The invitation surprised me, but Dr. Keskar explained that the Brahman gentleman who had sent the invitation was less orthodox in thought than Brahmans usually are; that he had been to England and America, thereby breaking his caste; but that he dressed in costume, observed the rites, and had duly performed all the ceremonies of purification, one of which is the eating and drinking of the five products, including the excretions, of the cow; so he had been received with no question among his people. The Brahman's wife greeted us shyly, bringing all the children to see us; but these did not sit with us at the meal, for Brahman women eat after the men have finished, the wife eating of the husband's leavings. There were several Hindu guests present, and we sat on the floor. Once, instead of the food being placed by my side, I thoughtlessly took it from the hand of the waiter, thus defiling the poor fellow, who was instantly compelled to take a purifying bath.

The eldest son of the family, a grown man, had appeared at the table in his white *dhoti* and shirt, and it was explained to me that the shirt was in deference to my feelings, for it is the habit of the Brahmans to dine in the *dhoti* alone.

Another curious custom which they observed was the surrounding of each leaf plate with a ring of water, and the placing of a morsel of food on the floor as an offering to the gods. This is the Hindu "grace."

Bidding the women good-by, in their own apartment, we joined the men in the drawing-room, chatted a while, and started homeward.

Squatting on his flat board seat our driver urged on the bullocks by tickling them with his toes, or twisting their tails, and all through the crowded bazaar his cry rang out frequently: "*A, gardi wallah, bahdsooday!* (O, driver of the vehicle, to the side!)"

A holy beggar—*fakir*—went chanting along as we passed, his flowing, unkempt hair and almost naked body proclaiming his profession.

Farther on, two Hindu gentlemen, having greeted each other, squatted down on the sidewalk for a cozy chat, sitting on their heels and bearing their whole weight on their toes.

As we passed the old fort we stopped to explore the interior, full of relics of ancient Hindu and Mohammedan life. I heard the legend of the woman who, with her unborn babe, was buried alive under the tower, as a religious sacrifice. I saw the crude, red-painted Kali, goddess of destruction, who stands with head bent forward. It is said that she swore no Englishman should ever set foot in the fort; and, when the English conquered and entered, the goddess bowed her head in shame and sadness, and has never raised it since. In the temple of the fort a very different and proud little Kali is decked in richest gold and silver and jewels, each of her eyes being a costly diamond.

On the outskirts of Sholapur we passed the relief tents, where people had fled from the plague. In Sholapur, a town of about seventy-five thousand inhabitants, thirty-six was at that time the average daily mortality, and the number steadily increased until the hot season.

So the days passed until, despite the cordial urging of the Sholapur people that I remain with them longer, I felt that I must begin my work in India. As the Government Surgeon of Sholapur advised me to go to Calcutta to see Sir Denzil Ibbetson, President of the Council, about a hospital appointment, I started on my journey across the whole breadth of India.

III

WAYSIDE SKETCHES

SUERNAMALA packed my valise with a few necessaries and many of her own ready tears, and, with the loud "Salaam!" of the children ringing through the air, I rattled away in the dust of the country road.

At one of the stations I climbed down from the train to observe more closely the scenes about me.

At all large railway stations a fenced-off yard is allotted to the third-class passengers, who, not having any idea of the time their train will start, or of the value of time in general, bring their blankets and other baggage the night before they wish to begin their journey and camp out in the station yard.

As our train stopped these fenced-in, would-be passengers crowded close to the gate. The guard let them out and they scurried for the third-class coaches. Pushing, pulling, crowding, huddling, shouting, they climbed aboard the train, and only when they had packed every coach to the limit of its capacity (the men in separate compartments from the women) did they seem contented. Gurgling hookahs, cigarettes, and small pipes made from leaves were produced (the women of India as well as the men smoke from early childhood), and, as the smoke issued forth in clouds, the tones sank to intermittent murmurs, and all was peace.

A young English soldier with a fair, good-humored face, in khaki uniform and with dark soldier cap set jauntily on one side of his head, was putting his Eurasian family into a third-class coach marked "For European Females." The coolie asked him a question and he replied with an impatient gesture: "Oh, go t'ell!" Then, seeing me, he added apologetically: "Beg pardon, Ma'am! But these fellahs, 'ow they do torment one!"

I had started again to board the train when I almost fancied I was having "visions," for I saw before me, among the motley Indian crowd, a young man in whose high-bred features, athletic air, natty gray suit, and Panama hat something spoke plainly of American university life. At the same moment he saw me and stopped short in his walk, staring hard. Then, flushing with pleasure, he rushed up to me.

"I beg your pardon, but you're a New Yorker, aren't you?"

"Yes; how did you know?"

"Why, that's easy; you've Broadway written all over you. I tell you, I'm glad to see you! A fellow gets awfully lonesome in this blasted country."

There was time for no more. The train bell rang for starting and I stepped into the coach, smiling a good-by to a homesick, boyish face.

Soon the Vindhya Mountains shut us in on every side, those wonderful piles of granite and syenite variously shaped as if, in ages past, giants must have hurled into the air immense boulders which fell on the flattened mountain tops in all sorts of positions until they took on the semblance of a great city standing strongly outlined against the heavens. I could see five of the boulders piled one on top of the other so delicately balanced that it seemed as if a child's hand could send them crashing to the valley below.

At one point the plain lay hundreds of feet below the track and the train passed through tunnel after tunnel. When I had counted twenty-five I thought of the old lady traveling through the Rocky Mountains who wondered what would happen "if the train should miss any of those holes."

Breaking my journey most pleasantly at Bhandara, where I spent a day or two at the hospitable home of Rao Sahib Rangrao, whose wife is Mrs. Keskar's sister, I then journeyed onward in company with Babu Rangrao, the eldest son of the house, who was on his way to the Calcutta Medical College, of which he was a student, and with Manakbai, the eldest daughter, returning, after her vacation, to the Calcutta High School.

In Bengal I was, for the first time, in the tropics of my dreams—moist and warm and luxuriant with bright-colored vegetation. Mud huts and huts of straw nestled among giant palm trees, every hut surrounded by its own garden of gay flowers. It lent a thrill to the scene to know that in the great forests we were passing the royal Bengal tiger stalked the deer and the wild elephant roamed in lordly freedom. Scores of the jungle tales I had heard in my childhood thronged upon me and held mad revel in my brain.

IV

THE CITY OF PALACES

According to Dr. Keskar's written request his friend Babu Atul Nag met me in Calcutta and we drove across the wonderful pontoon bridge over the Hooghly to the London Mission, where it had been arranged that I should make my home during my stay in the city.

When, during a pleasant interview next morning with Sir Denzil Ibbetson, he explained that in a government post the physician is not allowed to teach Christianity, I immediately gave up all thought of trying to obtain such a position, and decided to join some mission in need of medical services.

The charm of the "City of Palaces" held me a few days longer. Every afternoon we had a delightful drive along the broad Esplanade, through the stately Chowringhee Road, or about the magnificent public gardens.

Very noticeable was the white, wan look of every European I met in Calcutta, and the attitude of absolute ease assumed by them, the leisurely stroll of the pedestrian, the listless air of the gentlemen in carriages as they idly turned the sheets of newspapers, and the languid smile of the ladies as they passed each other in their evening drive.

The Bengalese appeared to me the finest looking Indian people I had seen, with their large, dark, lustrous eyes and European features, a bright-colored silk scarf thrown across the chest of the men and depending from the left shoulder adding a charming grace to their costume. The one defect in their appearance was the greasy look imparted by the generous quantities of cocoanut oil applied to their hair, which, unlike all the other peoples of India, they wear uncovered.

A Bengali wedding feast occupied one evening of our time. The Mission ladies and I, conducted by a servant with a lantern, groped our way through dark, narrow alleys, walking carefully to avoid the sewage gutters on both sides of the path, until we came to the low-roofed mud house of the bride's parents. Stooping low to enter the doorway, we passed through a dimly lighted room, stepping over dozens of naked, sleeping babies, left there while their parents enjoyed the festivities, and came out on the veranda of the courtyard, where the merriment was at its height.

The wedding ceremony was ended and the feast was in progress. We were smilingly greeted by the bride's mother, and, with a group of learned Babus—lawyers, clergymen, professors—we sat on the floor of the rug-covered veranda, eating with our fingers the delicious curry, rice, and sweetmeats placed before us, and watching the gaiety of the wedding guests.

Amid the loud report of firecrackers, the sputter and flare of Roman candles, and the bright light of red fire matches, young boys danced and frolicked about the courtyard to the music of an Indian band, and the shining, dark eyes and gorgeous costumes of the scores of guests crowded on the veranda lent added brilliance to the scene.

The bride herself, a slim, pretty girl of fourteen, surpassed all the others in splendor of costume. Her *sari* of pink brocaded silk was draped over an English blouse of red velvet and rainbow silk, whose name describes its color; while a massive silver ornament in her hair, two immense gold earrings in each ear, two or three gold and silver necklaces, several silver bracelets, gold finger rings galore, and silver toe rings and anklets helped in the bewildering display of light and color which she presented.

V

BENARES

ONE of the dreams of my life had been to see the Taj Mahal at Agra, and I took the opportunity to visit Agra before my return to Sholapur, stopping on the way at Benares, that "holy" city, supposed to rest on the point of Siva's trident and which for nearly three thousand years has been the center of Hindu learning and religious life.

At the station in Benares, an old Mahomedan guide with flowing magenta beard—the law denies an "old" man a license as a guide, hence the clever artfulness of the magenta color—entered my service and, knowing well what the *Sahib-log* (English people) wish to see, conducted me at once to the Ganges. There, from my comfortable seat on the deck of a boat, which muscular coolies rowed slowly up and down, I saw the amazing sights of that wonderful old city.

As we passed the Burning Ghat, three corpses were burning, each on a fagot pile three or four feet high, while the mourners sat on one side waiting to throw the ashes into the river, thus obtaining for their beloved dead the surety of heaven. A white-shrouded figure lay on the edge of the bank with the water lapping over it, and another was evidently undergoing preparations for burning. Less than a century ago that Burning Ghat had been the favorite place for *suttee,* when the dead went not alone to paradise.

"Hindus thinking va-a-ary good to die in Benares," remarked my guide, "but it being va-a-ary expensis!"

Judging from the appearance of the crafty-eyed priests and the loathsome *fakirs,* I could well believe that, once in their clutches, it would be difficult to escape, dead or alive, without paying heavy ransom.

From the river we walked to the various temples. As we passed the devotees, who were prostrating themselves before their idols, they drew their garments aside that they might not be polluted by our touch; and one old woman snarled savagely as my dress almost brushed against her.

VI

AGRA

IT was hot noonday when I arrived at Agra, the ancient capital of Akbar and of Shah Jehan. Just as at Benares, I found an old Mahomedan guide with a magenta beard; and we went immediately to the palace fort. There we wandered through a maze of rooms and courts and terraces and pavilions so immense and so gorgeously decorated that I was glad to come to the Pearl Mosque and feel the gentle influence on my spirit of the beauty, the purity, the solemnity of that matchless room of prayer.

From the marble terrace where Shah Jehan, grandest of all the Grand Moguls, used to go at sunset to gaze on the Taj Mahal and dream of the lovely woman who had made life for him a paradise on earth, I had my first glimpse of the Taj. Its great white dome and golden crescent shone through the trees, luring my mind toward the treat in store for me.

When the sun had passed the zenith I left the hotel for the Taj and walked the two miles alone, for I wanted no magenta-bearded guide to thrust his grotesque Urdu-English between me and this highest expression in the builders' art of man's love for woman.

In imagination let me lead all you who are lovers of the beautiful through the splendid gateway into the gardens of the Taj, that you may feast your own eyes on the glories therein!

Straight before you, but nearly a quarter of a mile away, gleams the cenotaph of the Begum Arjamund, so pure and beautiful that you stop for a moment to make sure it is of earth. It stands at the end of a long channel of sparkling water, running the whole length of the garden and constantly rippled by the series of tiny fountains it contains, each fountain throwing up a single spray.

On either side of the water is a row of Italian cypresses and, exactly halfway along, a marble terrace with garden seats tempts you to rest and gaze and dream, while all about you in every direction stretch the delectable gardens. Could even the Taj itself have a nobler setting than these well-ordered groves? The giant banyan spreads forth its branches and hanging roots; the stately palm tree reaches toward the heavens; and our familiar friends, the roses and the jasmine, clamber freely about among the rarest of trees and shrubs and flowers brought from far away to grace the scene; butterflies of extraordinary brilliance flutter among the flowers; while wee, striped squirrels play hide-and-seek among the trees and rocks; scarlet birds and birds of blue and of green form bits of darting color in the foliage; gorgeous peacocks sweep the soft grass and flash their bejeweled plumage in the sun; and the gladsome trill of the *bulbul*—India's thrush—fills your very soul with melody.

Passing on down the avenue of cypresses we draw nearer and nearer the mausoleum until it stands directly in front of us. From afar it was beautiful, but now, on closer inspection, it seems so exquisite that it might have been wrought from the frostwork on your winter window pane, flecked here and there with ethereal sunrise color. Clear-cut against the blue, blue sky it rises in all its peerless grace, and it is long before we can tear ourselves away from its fascination to visit the interior.

We enter the doorway and stand in a silent, softly lighted chamber. Delicately traced in the fairy mesh of the marble screen inclosing the tombs, a line of Arabic lettering tells us that "The Exalted of the Palace lies here," and that "Allah alone is powerful."

The dome has an echo unrivaled in strength

and purity throughout the world. With clear, rich voice the grave old Mahomedan caretaker strikes a few musical notes and, hark! the echo catches and transforms the sound into harmony, swelling, rapturous, which rolls on and on in lingering sweetness, until we involuntarily look up to see if some golden-throated choir be hidden above.

VII

SHOLAPUR AGAIN

SHOLAPUR again!

Mrs. Keskar met me at the station with a beaming welcome, the servants hurried my baggage into the *tonga,* and we rode home together in the cool morning air.

As I entered the compound all the children, lined up to greet me, sang in chorus their favorite song of welcome:

"Salaam! Salaam! Salaam! We offer you our greeting. Peace! May Jesus the Saviour bless you and with love and kindness daily watch over you! Joyfully we offer you our greeting. Peace! Salaam!"

I had been in Sholapur but a few days when a dark cloud settled over the compound. In the city the plague had mown down its victims with ever-increasing fury and now it came to our own compound. A sudden high fever attacked one of our baby boys, and, on close examination, we found a slight swelling under the child's right arm. In spite of every effort to save him he lived but a few hours. As he had slept in our room with his mother for several nights we carefully disinfected everything. Our people were panic-stricken; orders were given the cook to prepare meals in the open air; the children slept outside the buildings; and all precautions were taken to prevent the spread of the plague. Fortunately for us the rigid isolation and disinfection observed by Dr. Keskar saved our people almost entirely from the terrible epidemic, and it was but a short time before the immediate danger had passed away.

VIII

HYDERABAD

RESPONDING to an invitation from Mrs. George Nundy, wife of an Indian Doctor of Laws at Hyderabad, Deccan, I went to Hyderabad and spent a happy week at the beautiful home of the Nundys. There were interesting drives in the city, merry frolics with the children, tennis on the court, quiet walks in the moonlight, and several social festivities at the homes of the American missionaries at Secunderabad, a neighboring city, and of British and Indian Government people at Hyderabad.

In Hyderabad, you feel that you have stepped into the "Arabian Nights." The shining domes of great mosques and tombs, and the beautiful palaces of His Highness, the Nizam, rise above the blue and red and green and yellow houses of the city, whose roofs seem almost to meet over the narrow thoroughfares; a motley crowd of loud-voiced men and women shuffle slowly along in rainbow costumes; and scarlet and gold palanquins with curtains drawn close, indicating feminine occupancy, are borne past on the shoulders of coolies, who trot along at an even gait, chanting the "Palanquin Song":

"Ho, ho, hung!
Go ah gung!
Ho, ho, hi, hogan!"

Splendid equipages roll by, the gorgeous livery of the outriders showing that they belong to the establishment of some wealthy Nabob; hump-shouldered bullocks no bigger than Shetland ponies sturdily draw along their little two-wheeled carts; Arab horses in gay trappings, bearing lightly on their backs fierce men of the North armed with murderous looking weapons, dash through the throng clearing a wide path before them; camels with long-robed Bedouin riders pad through the streets; elephants trudge ponderously on their way with fringed and gilded howdahs on their backs and the voice of the *mahout* in their ears, or swing with pendulous motion behind the fence of their Fel-Khana (the "livery-stable" for the hundreds of Hyderabad elephants); and the air of the whole city is penetrant with the stale, sweet, oppressive odor of the Eastern bazaar.

Through the heart of the city rolls the wide river Musah until it comes out under the long *Bund,* the fashionable driveway of the place. On the outskirts of Hyderabad many large, white mansions, such as the Nundy residence, stand back from the highway amid a paradise of bloom; and huge guns on the crest of the hill, booming forth the hours as they pass, give the finishing touch to this wonderful old city.

The ancient Golconda fort and tombs and the famous diamond mines where the Koh-i-noor was found, and where *Sindbad the Sailor,* holding fast to the diamond-encrusted meat, was borne to safety by the roc, are a few miles out of Hyderabad, and, with the Nundys, we drove over to see them.

We reveled in the delicious coolness of the gentle Golconda hills, where the Nizam's court finds a pleasant summer retreat; marveled over the stonework of the fort and its underground passages centuries old; and, from the king's throne on the summit, had a fine view of the surrounding country. Then down we went to see the tombs, of which there are fifteen or twenty scattered over the wide plain, several of them very large and very beautiful.

My stay in Hyderabad was ended and I was having a thoroughly enjoyable visit with Dr. Ida Faye Levering of Secunderabad when news came that the Wesleyan Mission at Medak, sixty miles from Hyderabad, was sadly in need of a physician, and that they would like me to take the work. Miss Harris and Miss Posnett, missionaries from the Medak Mission, came to Secunderabad to meet me, and, when I learned from them that the medical superintendent of their hospital was obliged to go to England, leaving a district of five hundred square miles without a single qualified physician, the great need appealed to me, and I decided then and there to go to Medak.

IX

MY INDIAN HOME

MY life at the Keskar Orphanage was ended.

The farewell was a time of grief and hurry, but at last I tore myself from the arms of the dear children and ran to the waiting *tonga*.

On the way to Medak several *zenana* ladies traveled with me. As they walked from their covered carriage to the train they seemed a line of shrouded ghosts, for all wore the *bhourka,* a long, full, white cotton cloak reaching to the ankles, with hood covering the entire head including the face, leaving only an embroidered slit for the eyes. In the railway carriage, safe from male observation, they removed their "shrouds," and, behold! Silks and velvets of cream, dove-color, heliotrope, green, pink, blue, magenta, orange, and yellow, with gold and silver embroideries and ornaments, and precious jewels flashing a thousand light rays into my eyes, the heavy Eastern perfume pervading everything.

At Akanapett, the nearest station to the village of Medak, twelve miles farther on, Miss Harris met me. Breaking our journey by staying for the night at a nearby district dispensary of the Mission in the village of Ramyanpett, we started next morning in a bullock *tonga* for Medak.

The big white bullocks trotted along at a good pace over the rough country road through a landscape of rude, desolate charm. In former days this road was checked on the map of the Thugs as a place suited for their work. Nowadays a police *thana* marks the way every few miles along the Ramyanpett road to Medak, and there is little danger from savage men, though savage beasts still lurk in the deep woods and among the huge boulders and thick underbrush. Tiger, leopard, bear, or wolf frequently makes a night attack on the farmer's stock; and Miss Harris pointed out the lake where they drink. At that moment a colony of huge, black-faced, gray monkeys swung from a tree near the road to another and another at a prudent distance from us; but one mother monkey, too proud of her hairless, grimacing baby to lose such a chance of displaying his charms, climbed down from the trees, seated herself on a roadside rock, with legs hanging in front of her in a grotesquely human attitude, and clasped her offspring to her breast, her expression saying plainly: "Saw you ever such another?" We never had!

We passed the *Dhobi's* (washermen's) Stream, and there were the *dhobis* at work. Each *dhobi* selects a flat rock, places it in the stream, dips the clothes in the water, and slaps them vigorously up and down on the rock. This process is repeated until the clothes are clean; they are then wrung out and spread on bushes by the water side to dry in the hot sun. A careful folding serves very well for ironing, for the Indian clothes are only long, plain pieces of thin material.

A heap of boulders striped with red and white chalk marked a "holy place" of the Hindus; and almost at the end of our journey we passed the pathetic little Christian cemetery, its mounds leveled and protected with great flat stones from the ravages of jackal or hyena.

We reached the Mission settlement near the village of Medak just at the "dust hour"—the name the Indians give to the hour of sunset when the flocks and herds trailing homeward fill the air with such thick, white clouds of dust that a fog appears to have settled over the landscape—and passed directly from the *maidan* into the big white carriage gates of my new home in India.

As we entered the gates, the Indian school

children of the Mission came running with smile and *salaam* to welcome us. The English people of the settlement, of whom there were only eight or ten, met us with more dignity, but with no less cordiality.

The village of Medak, like the city of Hyderabad, is in the district of Hyderabad. This entire district—larger than the states of New York and Pennsylvania put together, and consisting of eleven and a half million inhabitants—is known as the "Nizam's Dominions," and is under the control of the Nizam of Hyderabad, a Musselman who, except the Sultan of Turkey, is the most powerful Moslem ruler in the world. Educated in England, the Nizam, although oriental in many ways, has broad, advanced ideas, and is loved and honored by the strange conglomeration of peoples that make up his subjects.

Indian rulers such as the Nizam have only limited power in their kingdoms. Without the consent of the British Government they cannot declare war or peace nor enter into agreements with other states, although they retain a certain military force of their own. In the case of the Nizam's Dominions, however, no European but the British Resident may reside in the state without special permission of the Nizam; and there is no British interference in the government except in case of excessive misrule.

Our Mission compound stands on high ground and is surrounded by a lonely, wildly beautiful landscape. On three sides, the *maidan* stretches off into the distance, its monotony broken here and there by rock or tree. Down below and just in front lies a placid blue lake where white and yellow lotus lilies float. Noble trees line the banks of the lake, the densely shadowing mango and banyan, the tamarind whose green, lacey foliage would delight the heart of a Corot, and the majestic date-palm towering high above them all against a sky shimmering with its intense blue and gold. Beyond are rice fields, more vividly green than the young rye of New England; and then, straight up for three or four hundred feet, rises a hill with immense boulders tumbled all over it, these boulders and the tall grass surrounding them sheltering hundreds of beasts of prey. The ruins of a stone fort and temple centuries old crown the summit of the hill, and at its foot are the little mud houses of Medak with a few structures of greater pretensions.

With striking distinctness in the midst of this scene stand out the white, well-constructed buildings of the Mission compound, set in the midst of pleasant, fertile gardens and fields.

In the large and comfortable bungalows each of us had a suite of two rooms, shared by the sparrows and bats which built their nests on a ledge just beneath the high ceiling of white-washed canvas, so that you almost felt you were camping out, the noise and dirt of the winged intruders adding to the realism.

The gardens were an entrancing mass of sweet-scented bloom and blazing color—red, orange, yellow, purple—with enough cool green and white to soften the beauty and add to it, while bright-plumaged birds and birds of somber hue called and sang everywhere and over the entrance gateway arched two pipal trees which rustled ceaselessly with a sound like gentle rain falling on the glistening leaves, deep green and silver lined. The pipal tree is the sacred tree of India, the bo-tree under which Buddha meditated, and under whose shade it is said no lie can be told.

My Indian nurses proved to be bright, clean, helpful young women, but Abbishakamma, chief compounder and chief Bible-woman, far surpassed them. Her wavy gray hair, which no amount of cocoanut oil would compel to smoothness, her dimples, and her merry brown eyes gave her a pleasing comeliness; while her general ability, her kindly cheerfulness, her never-failing loyalty, and her familiarity with the English

Medak Dispensary, vaccination day. Nurse Susanamma is helping Miss Wigfield and Abbishakamma is helping Dr. Munson.

language and with seven or eight of the Indian languages made her an invaluable assistant.

During prayer-service one morning, as Abbishakamma sat cross-legged on a large rug with a group of patients gathered about her, she talked to them with so much feeling and they listened with such unusual attention that I asked Miss Wigfield what the Bible-woman was telling them.

"That is Abbishakamma's favorite tale," replied Miss Wigfield. "It is of Elizabeth and her joy over her son. That one story, as Abbishakamma tells it, has brought us more patients, and has given the patients more faith in the Christian religion, than any other story in the Bible; for the supreme desire of every Indian woman is to have a son; and they would be glad indeed to worship any god who could grant them that desire."

India's need would appeal to a heart of stone. Some of the poor creatures who came to us for help had traveled for a week in a springless road-cart; others had walked sixty miles in the broiling sun. And the childlike attitude of the people toward us was pathetic. A dear old coolie woman said one night in the prayer meeting: "Oh, God, the white people have come to us from over the sea. They have given us much and helped us much. Give them strength to help us more!" They either feared us and tried to avoid us altogether, or they reverenced us as gods who held absolute power of life and death over them. I could stand being called their "grandmother," their "queen," or their "goddess," but when one of them would rub her forehead on my dusty shoes with the cry: "I am your slave; I kiss your feet!" I usually had an impulse almost irresistible to put one foot on her neck and fold my arms with a superior glance upward like the Roman gladiator. Again, when one buried her head in my solar plexus I felt that I must follow the example of the babies at home under like circumstances by squealing and grabbing a wisp of her hair. I knew, however, that this was but the oriental manner and meant much the same as a simple handshake in America.

I imagine that the strong races which swept down from the North to war against the people of Hyderabad District found them an easy conquest.

In appearance they are small and delicately built, especially the women, with brown skin and finely cut features, and their dress and general customs are those of the other Hindus of India.

The religion of the Dravidians, who originally possessed the Hyderabad country, was an almost unmixed form of devil worship; but now, the religion of the Deccan folk, their descendants, who call themselves Hindus, is a combination of devil worship, Hinduism and Buddhism.

As to character and conduct, the people have inherited docility, subtlety, timidity, and an attractive gentleness. In brief, if you will imagine the exact opposite of a typical American of the United States, you will have the East Indian as he appeared to me. The more I saw of India, the more I was convinced that

> . . . East is East and West is West, and never the twain shall meet,
> Till Earth and Sky stand presently at God's great Judgment Seat.

Fortunately for us and for them we do not expect them to become like us in the unimportant details. We do, however, want them to be not beasts of the field, but men.

X

THE RAINS

THE rains were late that first year at Medak and the peasants said that a hundred people must be kidnapped and killed and their blood allowed to float down the river to appease Gunga, goddess of rain. When the blood should reach a certain point, the anger of the goddess would depart and the rains would break. The attempt to secure the hundred people for the sacrifice threw the district into terror. Nobody went out alone after dark; and when, one night, a strange man came up and caught the hand of one of our schoolgirls who had wandered a short distance from the others out on the *maidan,* all the compound thought she escaped being a victim only through her screams, which immediately brought our coolies to the rescue.

Because of this lack of rain, the rice crop suffered and the people were heavy-hearted. Every evening and far into the night we could hear the unceasing song of the village women as they worshiped their gods, the monotonous hand-clapping and chanting, "Send us rain! Send us rain!"

But at last the rainy season came. It was necessary to protect our shoes and other articles of leather from the heavy mold which daily formed upon them, as well as from the white ants which worked their devastation at all times of year. Once, on returning from a three days' absence, I found the clay trail of the white ants on my best medical case, and, when I investigated, a long strip of its leather tore off and crumbled in my hand.

Other entomological specimens come with the rains. The *mantis,* green in color and two or three times as big as a grasshopper, looks like four animated leaves fastened together by the stems. Because of its habit of standing on its hind leaves and folding its front leaves together as if in prayer, it is called, "the praying one." Another, the "stick insect," measuring some three inches from tip to tip, and having three pairs of legs, I have frequently mistaken for a few wisps of dried grass, until, on brushing it away, I have been astonished to see it pick itself up and walk off. The locusts, reddish-brown with pink gauzy wings, are beautiful, a swarm of them having the appearance of a rose-pink cloud sailing through the air. But they are frightfully destructive, sometimes wreaking famine-producing havoc among the crops. This is easily understood when it is known that an army of locusts was at one time measured and found to be fifty miles wide, half a mile from front to rear, eighty feet high, and swarming densely.

It was after a hard shower that I saw from the dispensary door some animals hopping about in the wet road. At first glance I thought them wild hares, but on closer inspection found them to be frogs, the biggest I had ever seen.

"Yes," said the Indian nurses, awestruck, "every year they rain down from the sky."

The rain and wind of a fierce storm dulled all minor sounds when one midnight a cry, "Thieves!" woke everybody in the compound, and in less time than it takes to tell it we were flying hither and thither with lights and sticks and guns.

A burglar had broken into the hospital and stolen the head nurse's money and most of her clothes. He had rifled the storerooms throughout the compound, getting away with heavy booty. Afterward we learned that several of us had narrowly escaped death. The thief confessed in court that he had for several seconds bent over the sleeping form of the head nurse, prepared to stab her should she wake; and that, when Miss Posnett and I were searching for him in the hospital garden, we had come so near him at one time that he held his dagger prepared to kill us should we advance another step in his direction.

When the matter of the burglary was reported to the police of Medak, they, as usual, sat down apathetically, remarking, in regard to the matter, "What can we do?" But not so Mr. Hankin, their superintendent, an Englishman and one of the most competent police officials in India. When he saw no effort was made to find the culprit, he commanded that the salary of every one of his subordinates be withheld until the thief should be found. Instantly they set to work and within a few days the criminal was lodged in jail.

We were told that the burglar underwent the "tortures" before he would confess.

These tortures are worthy of the genius of the American Indian in that line. His jailers place red pepper in a man's eyes and violently rub them; they place scorpions in the orifices of his body; they thrust poison thorns into the orifices; they compel the prisoner to don leather trousers and then place in the trousers two wild, half-starved cats, allowing them to fight until they have torn themselves and the man's legs nearly to pieces.

The "cat torture" broke down the obstinacy of our burglar, and he told of an old, unused well in the jungle where he had hidden the goods.

There, sure enough, they were, though many articles were ruined.

The culprit was convicted and underwent severe punishment. His conviction would probably not have been so easy a matter had he possessed money, for the courts of Hyderabad District are corrupt to the core. Two *annas* (four cents) is the recognized price for a court witness, and for this he will perjure himself as long as anybody cares to listen.

After the burglary, a watchman was hired to parade the compound all night long. Every night, when I went to the hospital for midnight rounds, I stepped over him as he lay asleep on the doorstep with his lantern and stick beside him.

XI

OUR INDIAN FRIENDS

OUR Telugu *shastri* (professor), who used to come every day to teach us the language, was, as far as I can learn, a type of the Indian Brahman educated according to India's ancient ideals. His smooth-shaven face, his manner of dressing his hair—shaved all but the crown, and the hair of the crown gathered in a tight coil at the back—his plain, round, dark felt cap, and the flowing drapery of his white *dhoti* gave him a peculiarly feminine appearance. The umbrella he constantly carried had no special connection with rain or sun, but was a mark of rank, while the dark, heavy cord over his shoulder proclaimed that rank as highest—a "twice-born" Brahman. Always when he came to our bungalow we knew that under the closely fitting coat, which he wore in deference to our ideas of propriety, the cord lay over the right shoulder. This meant that he was "unclean," for he could not eat or worship until he had finished his morning's task with the no-caste Christians. If we chanced to meet him in the afternoon, the cord rested on his left shoulder and we knew he was sacred and untouchable.

When he came to teach us, he would retain his hat but politely remove his shoes, as he bowed low with a deep-voiced "*Salaam, Daura Sahni Gahru!*" (Greeting Honorable Madam!)

Among his own people the *shastri* was considered a profound scholar. He thoroughly understood Sanscrit and Telugu, and could recite in those languages verses by the yard; he knew every detail of the lives of the Hindu gods, but he never heard of Jupiter or Thor. He told me one day of a sea of milk which surrounds the "Northern World." When I asked him if he knew that the earth was round, he smiled scornfully:

"That is a belief for you Western people only; you have many strange beliefs!"

He was versed in Telugu art, but if we showed him a picture painted by an English artist—were it landscape or still life—he would turn it upside down, sidewise, and every other way, until at last he seemed satisfied—usually when it was upside down. Gazing at it long and attentively, he would remark gravely, "Very fine!" and put it down.

"What is it, Shastri Gahru?" we would ask.

"I don't know what it is," he would reply, "but it is evidently very fine work."

Some one has asked me why the Indian Brahmans, known to be people of refinement and education, do not establish universities of their own instead of importing Western teachers. Our *shastri* is the answer. From reading and questioning, I learn that there are probably few Indians, unless they have had Western teaching, more broadly educated than the *shastri*. He was progressive withal. Miss Tombleson, one of our missionaries, used to visit Hindu and Mahommedan houses of Medak, telling Bible stories and singing hymns. Always, when some new house opened its doors to her, the *shastri* was unquestionably pleased.

"But why are you pleased, Shastri Gahru?" she inquired one day. "You know I am working against your religion."

"Yes, I know, I know, but I like to see any good work thrive." This inconsistency is truly Hindu. Logic is no part of the Hindu's makeup. Should you say to him, "Black is white," he would reply, with bowed head, "If you say it is so, it is so! Why should not black be white?"

Another explanation of the *shastri's* attitude toward the Christians' work is that the Hindu has no wish to propagate his religion, and no hatred of other religions unless they interfere with his caste laws, which are his physical, mental, and moral life, and a sin against which is to him the only sin!

Even Mahomedan prejudice against our mission work is not nearly so strong as might be expected. From the time when the successful medical work of the mission had conquered his prejudice against the Christians, Syed-Shar-Tamal-ud-din-Ahmed-Kadri-Dadu-Badsha-Shar Sahib, the Mahomedan High Priest of Medak, whom we always affectionately called "Dadu Badsha," had been our firm friend, and by his loyal words and letters had won openings for our work into many hostile villages. At one time he gave a feast to our outcaste orphans, and, to show them his kindly feeling, he passed among them when they ate and with his own hand gave to each child a morsel of food, although to touch an outcaste Hindu is, to a Mahomedan, repulsive beyond anything we of the West can imagine.

There was much pomp and ceremony in the marriage festival of Dadu Badsha's daughter. Notwithstanding the wealth and high social position of our host, we were asked, according to custom when we Western people were invited to Indian houses, to bring our own food and chairs and table linen. This we did, not forgetting some pieces of pink toilet soap, for we knew we should be met at the *zenana* door by the High Priest's seven-year-old niece, who always begged for pink toilet soap.

"If I wash with your kind of soap," she would say, "I shall be made happy by becoming pink like you." We told her the soap would make no difference, and that her own color—a velvety brown—was much prettier, but she was not convinced.

One of the bits of soap was intended for Dowlat, a Telugu slave child, who used to plead as eagerly for it as did her mistress. Dowlat was sold to the *zenana* in her infancy; but the light-hearted child with frowsy hair and filthy clothing felt no discontent with regard to her lot in life. Having never known loving care, she probably never missed it. Then, too, the Mahomedans are not, as a rule, unkind to their slaves, merely indifferent. Among the three hundred and more persons who made up Dadu Badsha's household, there was, as is usual in Mahomedan domestic life, a pleasant democracy, the slaves and hired servants eating with the family and sharing sympathetically in the family joys and sorrows. Dowlat's only unhappiness came from her dissatisfaction with her complexion, which was of a shade but little less sooty than soot.

The wedding festivity proved altogether successful, although it grew a little wearisome when the Nautch girls had danced before us for an hour or two. These dancing girls are born into their profession, as is everybody in India, and are trained from babyhood to their immoral life, for the Nautch girls are wedded to the temples, that is, are prostitutes. Nevertheless, they suffer no reproach, are entertained with perfect cordiality in the houses of virtuous married women of every rank, and are treated with courtesy and respect by the men.

A young Nautch girl who came to our hospital for treatment, amazed when we asked her if she would not like to lead the pure life of a married woman, replied lightly, "Why? I am happy! Besides, I was born to the caste of temple girl. What can one do?"

At this wedding feast given by Dadu Badsha neither the dancing nor the songs were objectionable, and I learn they seldom are, unless men only are present. A fat, old person—the "Elephant," they called her—was the leader, and despite her weight and age was decidedly graceful. She trained well all the four younger women who accompanied her, often stopping in the midst of some sentimental song to snap out a criticism of their voices or gestures. She rolled her eyes, frowned, and smiled, wonderfully contorted her eyebrows and mouth, moved her hands and arms from side to side and over her head in gestures mild or passionate, while she sang in the harshest of cracked voices, and her ankle bells kept time—a slow, steady "clink-clink-clink"—to the music of sitar and drum. The dancers in shabby *saris,* but with costly jewels, chewed betel nut and had little laughing asides as if they were taking part in an undress rehearsal.

It was some variety when two Hyderabad girls took the place of the others. One, a girl of seventeen, with a handsome, wicked face; the other, a mite of seven, who clashed her anklet bells and danced heel and toe with the biggest of them.

The wedding gifts and the outfit of the bride and of the bridegroom were very rich and gay, for in India the groom is not, as at home, a secondary consideration. There were gold and silver and jewels, silks and velvets and fine linens, and some dainty hand embroidery wrought by the bride herself.

We women were permitted to see the bride, who sat on a crimson velvet couch, a crimson, gold-embroidered shawl completely covering her.

For forty days and nights she might see no face but her husband's; so when the elder sister allowed us to peep beneath the shawl, the eyes of the bride were downcast, but the mouth told us that she realized, with the childish delight of her thirteen years, her importance on the grand occasion. At the real wedding ceremony a day or two later, which I did not witness, the bride was represented by a man, and the entire service was with this proxy.

XII

AMERICAN THANKSGIVING DAY IN INDIA

IN India, America's Thanksgiving Day comes during the "melancholy days"; the hedge flowers have lost their brightest pink and blue, and the grass and trees look faded and yellow in an unlovely old age. The day was always, of course, a very ordinary one to everybody but myself.

With contrasting memories in my mind, let me tell you how I spent my first Thanksgiving Day in India.

Before the sun was well up, I tumbled out of my cot on the veranda and ran into my dressing-room. I had scarcely finished dressing when I heard on the other side of the door some one cough. As that is the usual way the noiseless-footed Indian servants announce their presence, I asked who was there. Venkiti, our assistant butler, made response, informing me that the other ladies had gathered at the table, and that whenever my Honor pleased I could be served with *chota hazrai.*

Chota finished, Miss Harris and I started in a native cart for Medak village to visit a woman who for days had been very sick. Curling our feet under us and sitting carefully, one in front of the other, in the middle of the cart to give leeway to our bobbing heads, we jolted over the rough road. Though the descent from these *bandies,* the only escape from which is over a high board at the back, appears more courageous than elegant, we were equal to the occasion, and, after a due exercise of forethought and gymnastics, found our feet solidly on the ground.

With bent heads to avoid the rafters, we entered the dark, close room where the patient lay. As is usual in any case of illness, the room was full of men and women. Ten women rushed to bring a light, or, rather, a hemi-demi-semi-light, for the Indian lamp gives the brilliant glare of an ordinary match with a London fog of smoke surrounding it.

The sick girl, staring at us with dazed, frightened eyes, crouched in a far corner with the beseeching cry, "Don't take me to the hospital!" We laughed her out of her fears—real fears to her, for the report had spread through the village that the English people had planned to offer a human sacrifice at the hospital so that luck

Indian carpenters at work

String bed of India, the common sleeping cot

might come to the place—and at last she drank the medicine we gave her and lay down to rest.

We were scarcely out of the house before an excited Brahman rushed up to us.

"Come quickly! Sitamma is dying!"

In his home, Sitamma, his child-wife of thirteen years, who had long suffered from an incurable disease, had been moved from the bed to the ground, for a Brahman must die on mother earth. Her face, once round and smiling, was pinched and drawn with pain, and the hollow eyes piteously besought our help as her arms reached out to us to come nearer. Her mother, scarcely more than a girl herself, stood by in silent despair, the tears flooding her eyes, and her *sari* drawn tightly over her mouth. Gathered about her stood four or five old Brahman widows, unjeweled and unjacketed, with shorn gray hair and in *saris* of coarse white muslin. A boy cousin of twelve, bewitchingly beautiful, his supple young body set off to advantage by a white loin cloth, his only garment, leaned against a pillar, watching, solemn-eyed, our every movement. Twenty other friends and relatives were there, all the women and children wailing loudly and the men standing silently, searching our faces for signs of hope.

Sitamma's family was one of the best in

Medak. Rich ornaments of gold and jewels hung about her neck, her arms, her ankles, encircled her fingers and toes, and pierced her nose and ears; and her clothes were of finest silk. But the room where she lay was devcid of furniture, mud-floored and rough-raftered. In a crevice of the dirty, white-washed wall was a crude, red-painted idol surrounded by offerings of fruits and vegetables, and with lamps burning before it. Over the crevice a number of cheap advertising cards were pasted, and, crowning all, a gaudily colored photograph of an English actor and actress.

When we had done what we could to ease the sick girl's distress and had passed out of the house, we could scarcely proceed for the number of people coming up, among them, Sitamma's great-great-grandmother, another Brahman widow, bent double and leaning on a stout stick for support, her shrill, cracked voice rising higher than all the rest in long-drawn wails for Sitamma.

Back to the dispensary and hospital duties!

One of our hospital in-patients was a baby boy who had been so terribly mutilated by a pariah dog that he almost died before our long fight at last brought strength and health to the little body and a crooked smile to the red lips.

Two others were victims of the habit among Mahomedans of giving their children opium in large quantities. Of these patients, one boy was three years old, the other, four months, but there was little difference in their size. They greatly improved under treatment, and the elder could, when he left the hospital, waddle weakly about on his spindle legs, his big goblin head rolling considerably but containing on its anterior aspect a Cheshire cat expression.

A patient suffering with rheumatic fever of the arm had been told by a *hakim* that the pain was caused by poison thorns placed in her flesh by evil persons. To prove his diagnosis, he had shown her a handful of thorns which he pretended to have extracted from her arm during his examination of her. Nothing we said could change the girl's conviction that the thorns had been in her arm, only she wondered why she felt no better after their extraction.

Another case was that of a young woman who came to us with acute indigestion. When I made my rounds she asked: "How soon can you cut me open and take it out?"

"Take it out!" I repeated. "Take what out?"

"Why," she exclaimed, "you are a doctor; you have felt my pulse; surely you know what ails me! A priest told me that an enemy had placed the stone image of a god in my stomach, and I want that stone image cut out!"

We pleaded and reasoned with her all in vain. She left the hospital in search of some doctor who would cut her open and take out the god.

The five-year-old son of a Mahomedan official of Medak was one of our most grateful patients. We had been obliged to lance two boils on his leg, and, at the last cut, the child raised both arms to heaven, and, turning his tear-stained face upward, cried out, "Oh, God, God, what a sick man am I! Why hast Thou deserted me? Relieve me of this agony! Take me to Thyself! I can bear no more!" When a soothing dressing had been applied, however, the pain vanished and he smiled through his tears, promising magnificent presents for us all.

Far more cause for gratitude had the bonny boy of two, whose eyelid healed well although it was gashed in half a dozen places by the horn of an angry bull. Mercifully, the eye was spared. Every day, while I applied medicine and dressings to his eyelid, the wee lad howled himself hoarse; and every day my eyes were wet with tears over the plump, naked, brown baby who had to suffer such pain, and who, after the dressings were ended, would spring with a tearful smile straight into my arms, and lay his loving, forgiving head on my shoulder as I carried him to his mother.

Amadbhi, a Mahomedan girl-wife, had been for weeks a patient in our hospital. We allowed her young husband, who waited impatiently for her recovery, to make his home on our front veranda—a neat, little bachelor home, all in the space of a few feet, with a blanket for a bed, his own turban for a pillow, a clay lamp, and a little pile of pots and pans for cooking his simple meals. He was always spotless in appearance, for there was a lake close by and on the flat stones he pounded his garments clean, hanging them to dry on the bushes along the bank. Several times a day, Amadbhi donned her *bhourka,* thus hiding her face from all other men, and crept around to cheer her young husband in his solitude, until at last she recovered and they went their happy way.

A charming Mahomedan princess of Hyderabad, who had been at various times a patient of ours, made a pretty picture as she reclined on her bed with her pet fawn—a wide blue ribbon tied in a bow about his slender neck—snuggling against her. This princess gave us, in gratitude for treatment received, land in one of her own villages on which to build a chapel, and free permission to preach Christianity throughout the village.

We had a young Arab woman as a patient in our hospital. The Arabs are a manly race, with the deserved reputation of being "a faithful friend and a dreaded foe." Their costume is very picturesque; a short, striped skirt reaching barely to the knee, a turban to match, the end streaming to the waist at the back, long coat of white muslin, low shoes with toes turning back in long points toward the ankle, and belt-sash stuck full of pistols and dirks ornamented with gold and silver and jewels. Every day the husband and brothers of our Arab patient came to see her, one of the big fellows always sitting outside her door at night to keep watch over her sleep.

One of these Arabs asked me if I would open an abscess for him. Calling to mind the shrinking, cowering Hindu when anything surgical is in evidence, I warned the Arab, as I picked up my knife, to sit quite still, and added in soothing tones: "It will hurt but a second!" He smiled scornfully.

"I am not a child, Doctor Mem Sahib; I do not fear pain!"

And he smiled on, never flinching, during the operation.

The idol of all these Arab giants and of their kinswoman was her baby Esau. Like a group of children, they would gather about and watch intently every time little Esau was fed his prepared food from a nursing bottle.

"This matter of bottle-feeding," said the father, "is from your country. No one in India would have thought of it!"

Rama, a Brahman boy of thirteen, with delicate hands and feet like a girl's and with an affectionate, gentle manner and an engaging smile that sent him straight into the hearts of all who knew him, suffered with diseased feet so that for two years he was altogether unable to walk. His father, a *hakim* (Indian herbalist), who had vainly made every effort to cure the boy, hated our Mission from both professional and religious jealousy, and it severely humbled his pride when he brought his son to our hospital and begged us to attempt his cure. The serious operation we performed was, happily, successful, and when the boy could run about as merrily as any other laddie, the father seemed to put aside his last bit of resentment and suspicion in regard to us.

When I visited Rama's room the evening before he left us, he sat on his bed surrounded by his adoring father and his four adoring uncles—Rama is the only boy in all the family—who listened with admiration while he sang in his shrill voice the old Hindu songs they love.

Notwithstanding the Brahman fashion of wearing his hair—shaved all but the crown—and the wide red and yellow caste marks on his forehead, Rama looked almost beautiful as, with shining eyes, he cuddled close in his arms the English doll we had given him, a blue-eyed lady in a pink dress, to whose finery he had added garlands of white jasmine. As I entered the room, Rama and the elder gentlemen rose with profound *salaams* and the boy laughingly threw a long jasmine garland about my neck and made his dollie *salaam* to me.

As I patted the lad's head and tweaked the long, sacred lock hanging from his crown, he laid his cheek against my arm and murmured in his pretty oriental way: "To-morrow I shall be at home and very happy, but I shall miss the dear white ladies. When you say good-night with those loving words and caress me thus, a great peace like the soft wings of a bird closes over my spirit and I sleep well and sweetly."

More and more did I wonder, as the days went by, that we had patients from any other place than our own village of Medak, because of the difficulties and peril in reaching us.

Ramavva, a high caste Hindu woman, used

to come to us every few months for treatment, caring nothing that, to do this, she had to ride alone for three days on the back of a buffalo through the rough, lonely jungle.

When she arrived at the hospital one night, she told us an incident of her journey:

"You know," she began, "that I have learned many Bible stories and Christian hymns here at your hospital, and at home I tell my family the tales and sing the hymns for them. By the tale which I will now relate, you will perceive that I am a Christian at heart, though I implore you to tell no one, for I wish to have no domestic difficulties.

"As I journeyed toward the hospital yesterday, I was passing through the woods when I saw a camp of Dacoitics (Hindus who are born to the caste of robber and murderer) among the rocks. They were very near, and I feared they had already heard my buffalo trampling and that I was lost. Then I remembered the words of the Christians, and, jumping down from my bullock, I knelt on the grass and prayed: *'O Jesu Swami* (Lord Jesus), save me!' When I arose, I looked, and behold! the wicked men had not noticed my approach, so I quietly led my buffalo a roundabout way and came on in safety."

Ward rounds ended, I went to the dispensary.

Kadrabhi was the first to greet us. Kadrabhi was a Mahomedan woman of rank and, therefore, had to keep *gosha*. Too poor to own a curtained *zenana* bandy, she would come afoot in the darkness of the early morning and out again when the sun had gone.

Then the patients came in force, plucking our sleeves, crowding upon us, and shouting their symptoms in loud tones, until we laughingly covered our ears with our hands and our nurses brought them to order.

A large, muscular woman showed us a recent fracture of the wrist, with hand swollen to a ball. We removed the peacock feather which she had tied about her wrist for good luck, and prepared for treatment. Suddenly terror seized her, and before we could stop her she had fled.

Another woman who had been holding over her face the corner of her *sari* drenched with blood, removed the cloth, disclosing a hideous mutilation. Her husband, to punish her for infidelity, had, as is customary in such cases, cut off her nose.

One of our coolie women brought to us her babe.

"Will you burn her stomach, please, Honorable Doctor Madam?"

In the Medak Dispensary. Offerings of a grateful patient (child), sheep and garlands. Mother in *bhourka*. Dr. Munson holds child on her knee.

Mahomedan Madas bringing gratitude offering of sheep garlanded with flowers. Dr. Munson seated.

"Why?" I asked in amazement, for the child was in perfect health.

"Oh, it will keep her well. My stomach was burned when I was a baby, and see how well I am," and she proudly displayed three wide ugly scars on her brown skin.

Will the Indian *hakims* ever realize for how much their ignorance is responsible?

A child was brought to us with her eyelids nearly burned through for a simple inflammation. When I asked her mother what other treatment the eyes had received besides the burning, she replied: "The *hakim* has done all things known to him. The last treatment was red pepper to be rubbed into the eyes every hour."

A day later came a baby boy struggling with agony in his mother's arms, the delicate flesh of his abdomen so deeply burned that the bowel slightly protruded and made his death inevitable.

Five-year-old Mahomedan Madas was brought to us with his cheek torn open from nose to ear and deep down to the bone where one of the vicious Indian ponies had bitten him. The village *hakim* had put foul dressings on the wound till it was thoroughly poisoned and the child was dangerously ill. Every day he had to undergo a very painful treatment, but he seemed to know we were trying to help him, for only a low moan now and then betrayed his suffering. Madas must have felt that the last Thursday in November was a day of special gratitude, for that morning he, with his mother and aunt, walked into the dispensary, leading by a rope of grass a large black sheep garlanded with wild flowers. The boy bowed to the ground in his *salaam,* and as he placed the leading rope in my hand, lisped: "Because you made me well, dear Doctor Mem Sahib, I now with deep gratitude present to you my sheep."

We heard a sound of wheels and a loud shuffling in the courtyard as a *zenana bandy,* covered over with plaited straw and closely curtained, emptied its contents. Whenever a *zenana bandy* emptied its contents, I felt inclined to doubt the old axiom, "No two bodies of matter can occupy the same space at the same time." After the patient, an old lady with chronic indigestion, had been helped out, there slowly clambered to the ground women with their head covering thrown back as if in enjoyment of the untainted air of heaven; ornaments covering nose, ears, forehead, neck, arms, ankles, fingers, and toes, chinking heavily as they walked; and, in almost every instance, plump babies sat astride their hips. Then there tumbled out small boys in red fez and long, white coat and trousers; and girls in gay pajamas and short over-garment of coarse net, their bodies loaded with ornaments like their elders. Bonny youngsters these who seized our hands and danced around us begging for a rose or a doll or a sweet, their black eyes looking out of chubby olive faces, full of a winning impudence. But they had learned courtesy, too, for nothing was received without a clear-voiced "Salaam, Doctor Mem Sahib!" and a graceful bend from the waist, as the right hand was pressed to the forehead.

Then came the usual equipment of a patient who expects to remain in the hospital: Brass cooking utensils of every imaginable size and shape, rice, clarified butter, vegetables for curries, other foodstuffs, and then a pile of wraps and bedding.

In these matters our hospital had to depart from strict Western discipline. Unless the family, or at least one or two members of it, had been allowed to move in with all the paraphernalia necessary to light housekeeping, we should have had no patients in our hospital. In a way it was a help, because, never having enough nurses and other hospital assistants, we resigned much of the care of the patient to her family with, of course, careful supervision by our own nurses.

Very different from the Mahomedan children

was the naked Hindu boy close by, who, with the sacred lock of his crown hanging listlessly from his shorn head, shrank behind his mother with a wail of fright at the strange white faces.

Another fracture and another *hakim* treatment! The boy's hand was badly swollen, the arm bound in a vise, and the fracture not reduced at all. This time the sufferer was a Brahman boy, and, when the arm was neatly dressed and bound, his mother, who had accompanied him, inquired: "How can he bathe?"

"Let him bathe the rest of his body, but leave that one arm," I replied.

"Then he cannot eat," she argued, "for he is a Brahman." And she departed with a look on her face which plainly said, "Fracture or no fracture, that arm shall be washed before he touches a morsel of food." I have no doubt that twice daily our dressings were soaked with water if not entirely removed.

At the far corner of the men's veranda crouched a tall Hindu, now fingering his necklet of snakes' vertebræ and now a written charm—*mantrum*—in a brass box tied around his arm. His eyes were wide with terror and his lips scarcely able to frame a request to have an abscess cut. His baby son had just been cured of an abscess covering nearly the whole leg, and the man's confidence in our healing powers had overbalanced his fear of the knife sufficiently to bring him to us.

"Now, have courage," I exclaimed, "and it will be over in a second."

"Oh, no, oh, no!" he howled. "Give me sleeping medicine as you gave to my little boy. I have no courage; I shall die!"

So a whiff or two of chloroform, a quick cut, a simple dressing, and all was over, and the grateful fellow pressed his forehead to our shoes.

"And how did you say I am to take this medicine?" inquired an old woman to whom I had already given clearest directions in my best Telugu.

"Four days, eight doses, one dose every morning, one dose every evening."

"Salaam, honorable lady, I am your slave; it is four doses and every evening I shall drink."

"No, eight doses, four days."

"Yes, my honorable grandmother, I kiss your feet; I shall drink in the morning and not in the evening, for eight days."

"No," desperately. "Now listen! Four days, eight doses, every day two doses, one in the morning and one in the evening. Good-by! Salaam!"

"Salaam, my queen of queens! I will do as

you say and will not drink in the morning or in the evening, but in the noonday for eight days."

And off she went, repeating and re-repeating the directions with her own variations, and I could only feel grateful that the remedy was harmless and her mode of taking it mattered little.

A few more malarias and bronchitises, two major surgical operations, and then breakfast, which consisted of fruit, followed by curry and rice and always tea.

After breakfast came the noonday rest-time, when all the Indian world sleeps and the very insects seem to hold their breath.

Nap ended, I went out to tea, which, like *chota hazrai,* was a simple meal—fruit, bread, cakes, jam and tea.

Another look at the patients, and then I galloped off to make my afternoon visits in the village, my *syce,* with one hand on the stirrup, running beside the horse.

In the West, what a record in cross-country running the Indian *syce* would make!

Our Davadass, a man of fifty years, has run one hundred miles in two days—fifty miles, a night's rest, and then the other fifty. It was a pleasure to watch him as, with *dhoti* bound tightly around the loins, he would run on and on

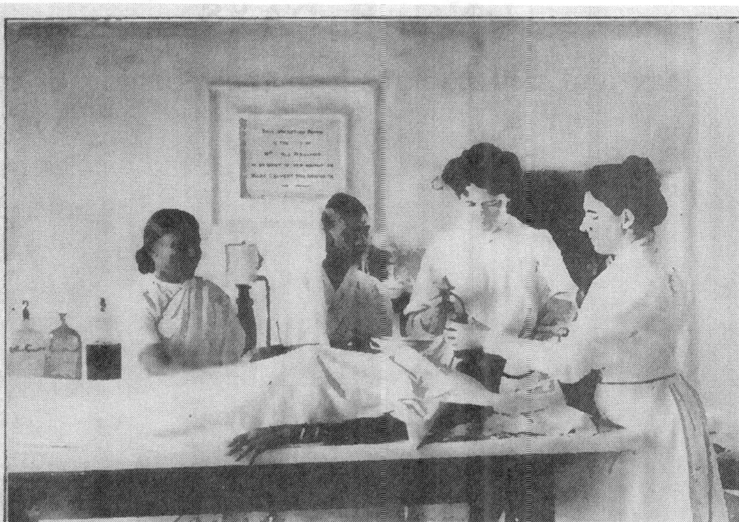

Dr. Munson operating in Medak Hospital

Corner of medical ward, Medak Hospital. Dr. Munson with head nurse and patients.

with swift rhythmical gait that never seemed to weary.

Dinner was at half past seven—my Thanksgiving dinner! The turkey at home was represented by jugged goat which, though not so strongly flavored with circus posters as might be expected, required some skill and experience in the art of mastication. I looked wistfully on while the others ate with relish such barbarities as *tahku* (the Indian hot flavoring agent), *kahram curry* (it is a wonder there was any skin left on their tongues!), and the native vegetables which all tasted alike to me and all like slippery elm. But then I reflected with pride that the ancient Romans did not surpass us altogether in luxury of diet, for one evening we dined on peacock and ants' eyes. The peacock was no less palatable because the entire bird cost but sixteen cents; and the ants' eyes were no less highly valued because we had them at every meal—with the rest of the ants' "material organized substance" (Venkiti always forgot to cover the sugar bowl).

As for the peacock, when I learned what the poor thing had suffered before its death, my conscience smote me for having eaten it. That the birds may not be able to find their way back to the woods, the trappers sew their eyelids together, not always careful to sew the eyelids only; frequently the eye is pierced.

After dinner, I went again to the hospital, had a few friendly chats with the patients, and then came in to study for a while under the light of the big *punkah* lamp (a lamp with a shade surrounding all the sides and curving over the top, protecting it from the breeze of the *punkah*).

The jackals howled vociferously; the flying-fox gave every now and then a shrill, hissing whistle; the night owls hooted mournfully, and the frogs and crickets joined their voices to the chorus. Everything was so different from home—the loneliness, the eternal summer, the heavy responsibility! I was too busy in those Indian days for a severe attack of homesickness, for every minute had its pressing duty which could not be put aside for any little "joy in sorrow" of mine. Nevertheless, I felt sometimes that the world was very thick through, and the word "America" sent an almost painful thrill down my spinal column. I liked my work; I liked India; but my altogether lovely home country grew dearer to me every day.

East, West,
Home's best!

But the air was fragrant with the breath of jasmine and roses and oleander, and the moonlight was glorious. I was glad indeed to see my dear "Moon-girl's" friendly, comforting glance. In India, the Moon-girl does not hold up her head in her proud American way, but gazes ever downward. Astronomers may call it "diurnal libration," or what they will, but I know she bows her head in sadness for that sad land.

So the day ended, and, creeping into my veranda cot, I forgot Thanksgiving Day in foreign lands and all other forms of self-pity, and slept dreamlessly under the Moon-girl's tender gaze and the soft caress of the night breezes.

XIII

CHRISTMAS

I HAVE already described the charm of the Christmas season in India; the balmy air, the wealth of garden bloom, the green trees and greener grass giving no hint of the cold, white Christmas season of the West.

My first Christmas at Medak was just such a day as India expects at that time of year—not a cloud in the sky. From the dark of Christmas Eve to the dawn of Christmas Day, the boys and girls and coolies came in sets and sang Christmas carols near the veranda where we lay in bed, only stopping when a present was thrown to them.

The morning service was held at the *dharmatsahla,* a sort of hostelry whose generous size helps much toward the accommodation in the compound of the thousands of Christians from the district outside of Medak who foregather with the Medak Christians on any special occasion.

It was an inspiring scene when all those Indian Christians, in their gaily colored clothes and with eyes and teeth and jewels shining bright against the brown of their faces, waved their arms above their heads, while they sang in loud, jubilant chorus:

> Victory to Jesus!
> Victory to Jesus Christ!
> Victory to the Lord Jesus Christ!
> May His Kingdom come! *Amen!*

At the school we had games and a merry feast with the children, when we all sat about on the floor, eating with our fingers from plaintain leaf plates.

Then we superintended the festivities at the hospital. Every arch and pillar of the long hospital veranda surrounding the courtyard was decorated with Japanese lanterns and garlands of flowers. All the boys and girls had pretty presents; and though some of the child invalids could not be moved from their beds, they stretched their wasted arms for the big doll or the toy horse with all the longing of the others.

At night, after a huge bonfire and the distribution to the Christians of the Christmas-tree presents, we again sat down on the floor and ate with the Indian people. Then Mr. Posnett, their beloved "Padre Sahib," showered sweetmeats among them, and the day's festivities were ended.

XIV

DREAM DAYS AMONG THE HIMALAYAS

WHEN we considered the pros and cons of a hot summer on the plains, the cons predominated and we decided to go to Mussoorie and Simla.

On our journey, we had the whole railway coach to ourselves, and, lounging in kimonos, we were very comfortable in spite of the heat, the ovenlike breeze being cooled by its passage through grass window blinds saturated with water.

As we neared the Ganges, we passed a band of pilgrims, most of them sick or aged, filing through the dust of the roadway. Some of these weaker ones crept painfully along by themselves; some leant on the arms of their stronger companions; and all struggled onward with the hope of washing in the sacred Ganges before their death.

At Dehra Doon we came to the last railway station before the ascent to Mussoorie. After a refreshing lunch and rest at the hotel, a four-mile drive through the Doon, one of the most beautiful and fertile of Indian valleys south of Kashmir, brought us to the base of the mountains; and then came a ride of eight miles up the steep mountainside, in a *dandy* (a cushioned, boat-shaped chair carried on the shoulders of four coolies).

The moonlight brought out clearly the sharp, black peaks high overhead, and threw colossal shadows on the solemn valley below. The only sound that reached us was the pattering of the coolies' bare feet, or a sudden burst of talk or song or laughter among them. Round and round the mountain we curved, its rocky walls reaching straight up for hundreds of feet above our narrow path, and straight down, blotted out in a yawning chasm of darkness below. Then came the quiet coolness of the denser wood, and my head gave several warning nods; so, half-asleep and half-awake, I passed through that seductive green to the heights beyond.

There at Mussoorie, where the season was like England's June-time, we passed delightful days among the pines and woodland flowers, while, above the clouds high overhead, the majestic, snow-crowned Himalayas, range on range, swept off into space.

Then on we went to Simla, Kipling's paradise on earth.

As at Mussoorie, we spent most of our time dreaming the days away "under the deodars," but we also enjoyed wandering about the village searching out the places filled with memories of *Kim* and other friends.

XV

BACK TO THE PLAINS

DORA CHATTERJEE, my college friend, whose sister, Mrs. Nundy, I had visited in Hyderabad, had invited me to her home in Hoshiarpur, so, arranging to meet the English girls on the way back to Medak, I went to Hoshiarpur. Dora's cousin, a young Indian prince, met me at Jullundar, and we chatted pleasantly until Dora's father, Dr. Chatterjee, the well-known scholar and philanthropist of the Punjaub, arrived to take me to Hoshiarpur, some twenty-five miles distant. As we bowled over the smooth, hard road, as well kept as a city mall, Dr. Chatterjee told me fascinating tales of his boyhood days when he was a Bengali Brahman, and of the bitter persecution he suffered when he became a Christian. The long drive seemed scarcely to have begun before it ended and we were at Hoshiarpur, where my dear college mate and her charming mother and sisters greeted me most cordially.

The Chatterjee homestead was a fine old place,

indeed, a large, white bungalow encircled by wide verandas and set far back from the road amid shade trees, orchards and gardens.

The days passed swiftly and pleasantly. Every morning Dora and I rose with the sun, and, after working most of the day at Dora's hospital in the city, we spent the early evening in one festivity or another—a tennis or badminton party, a drive, a dinner or tea, calls, and usually two or three combined, for there are many English people of the Civil Service stationed at Hoshiarpur.

It was hard indeed to leave my friends and the happy life of the Punjaub to begin the long, hot journey southward.

Sightseeing is, I think, usually more interesting than comfortable, and my experience in Delhi was no exception to the rule. The place was like a furnace, but fascinating in the curious mixture of growth and decay that marks this old city which was for so many generations the capital of the Mogul emperors.

Chandni Chauk, the "Street of Light," might be termed also the "Street of Life," for I never before saw or heard such a swarm of bees in butterfly garb and human form as that which makes this street one of the busiest in India.

An English soldier took me through the fort

Dora Chatterjee

then used as barracks for the English army. Though ruinous far beyond the fort at Agra, it was decidedly imposing, and the *Diwan-i-Khas,* or Private Hall of Audience, was unique in the beauty and taste of its gorgeous ornamentation. Open on all sides to the palms and the sunshine and the penetrating blue of the Indian sky, with graceful Saracenic columns and arches, richly carved, gilded, and inlaid, until the whole room is one blaze of gold and silver and jewels, flashing blue, red, purple and green, it formed a fit setting for the famous Peacock Throne which once stood there, and you could not wonder that it inspired the distich written in Persian on the ceiling:

> If on earth be an Eden of bliss,
> It is this! It is this! It is this!

The Jumma Musjid at Delhi, the largest mosque in the world, is very majestic with its white marble ornamentation on red sandstone; but I had seen the Pearl Mosque at Agra, which is built on somewhat the same plan; and the Pearl Mosque is so much purer and lovelier that I could part without regret from the Jumma Musjid.

Although it was noon when I left the Musjid, I drove eleven miles to the outskirts of the city, where, in the midst of a wilderness of pathetic ruins, rose that wonderfully carved shaft of red sandstone—world-renowned and rarely beautiful—the Kutb-Minar!

The drive back to the city was cool and restful, and I felt quite refreshed when I resumed my railway journey.

The English girls had rejoined me and we had dined at one of the stations when, as we re-entered our coach, we saw that we were not alone. In one of the "upper berths" a deer-eyed, brown woman peeped shyly out from her *bhourka.* Close to her breast she held a chubby two-year-old boy, who seemed inclined to cry at sight of us. Just then the anxious face of a young Mahomedan gentleman appeared at the window.

"Madam," said he in English, "you must care my wife because she has small child; because of small child, you must care. I commit you, Madam, I commit you!" and he hurried away as the train started.

Of course, we helped the timid creatures down to a safer level, and did our best to make them feel more at ease.

At Aurungabad station we left the train to make the trip to Ellora Caves. It was a long, hard journey in the hot noonday up the sun-dried, lonely ghats to the caves. We frequently relieved our ponies by walking, and every few minutes we sat down to rest. But the heat and the weariness were forgotten in our wonder and admiration for those vast, underground temples which, gouged and chiseled ages ago out of the solid rock, extend for a mile and a quarter along the face of the hill.

As I stood beside the Buddha in the "Carpenter's Cave" my waist came just to his knee, and I climbed up on the knee and sat there for a while to give the rest of our party an idea of the size of the image.

In the Brahmanical caves, the old legends that Mrs. Keskar had told us came swarming back upon me. The handsome, mischievous boy-Krishna was there, and there was Hanamanthadu, the Monkey-General. Gluttonous Ganesh, fat and kindly, with his absurd elephant-head, gazed blandly at us over his broken tusk; heroic Rama and his gentle Sita wandered through the enchanted wood; Siva of the frowning brow slew his enemies or peacefully played chess with his terrible wife, Parvati; and amorous Vishnu whispered his love-tale into the ears of Lakshmi, his beautiful consort.

Every line in these underground marvels was clear and accurate. Each petal of the lotus-flower stood out in bold relief; and the pillars in the great vaults were as straight and smooth as if planed by an expert carpenter. Nothing but a visit to the place itself could convey its atmosphere, the dark corners where bats cling to the ceiling or object, with sharp squeaks, to being disturbed, the earthy dampness, the deep, deep recesses rank with the wild beast odor of the hyenas, wolves, and leopards, which frequently take refuge there, and the filthy old priests who keep the place in order and haunt your every footstep begging for *bakshish*.

Not only does the Nizam of Hyderabad issue his own coinage and stamps, but also collects customs at the boundaries of his territory. The wearisome "red tape" of this customs procedure after our midnight landing at Mirzapally station, and the five hours' jolt over rough roads while our heads tumbled sleepily about and we hung desperately to the *tonga* to keep from being thrown to the ground, made our compound seem a veritable Eden as we entered its gates in the freshness of the early morning and received the hearty welcome of our people.

XVI

WE GO A-TOURING

RESPONDING to an urgent call from Ellareddypett to come there with medicines, we made a medical tour of a week to Ellareddypett and other outlying villages of the district.

Our *chaprassi* (messenger and guard), fully armed, went a day in advance of us, as he always does in case of touring, to get the permission of the *patel* (head man) for our coming into his village; to arrange for the location of the tent, for the food and other supplies; and to hire an Indian band which should emphasize our worth and importance by parading the streets every night from sunset to dawn with instrumental din and loud shouts of, "The white lady doctors are coming! Bring your sick! Bring your sick! They will be cured!"

Half a day after the *chaprassi's* departure went our assistants, servants, and equipment to make everything ready for immediate work on our arrival. Then early next morning, Miss Tombleson and I left the compound in the "box *bandy*," bound for Ellareddypett, where our way had been prepared.

I am a long-suffering individual with regard to modes of travel, various or curious, but then and there I decided that, when there should be no other vehicle at my disposal except our "box *bandy*," the motion of which resembled that of a storm-tossed ship in a cross-current, I should risk the foot blisters and heat stroke of pedestrianism in India!

When, after long hours of rattling and bumping along the way, Miss Tombleson had grown sober in the eyes and white about the lips, and I had passed through the stage immediately following that, the sun was low enough to risk walking and we gladly crawled out of our discomfort and stretched our cramped limbs luxuriously.

At Nargareddypett our evangelist and his wife entertained us to the best of their ability, but the dear people were sadly flustered in trying to supply the needs given us by the complicated domestic life of the West. We had brought our own loaf of bread and bottle of milk and, after long search and much scrubbing, our hostess produced two battered enameled plates and two sea-shells. That was all, but we managed very well as, seated on the plank which protected us from the mud floor, neatly and properly washed with cow-dung, we took turns at tearing off chunks of bread which we soaked in the milk and dipped up with the shells.

Our weariness from the day's travel made our narrow string cot seem like a state bed of softest down. The cot had been placed under the window of the little room where until midnight the village Christians sang their evening hymns—flats a specialty and sound their chief object; the snores of the *chaprassi* and *bandy* driver from the veranda near us came plainly to our ears; and the squealing and grunting of pigs from their pen six yards away mingled with the sudden snort of an astonished bullock or buffalo that, wandering idly about the grounds, had discovered on close investigation that our faces were not a midnight meal. Nevertheless, we turned over—simultaneously of necessity—and slept like babies till the morning sun shone full on our eyes.

Another meal of bread and milk and we started again toward Ellareddypett. With yesterday's experience fresh in our mind, we decided to walk and trudged on for an hour and a half, when the hot sun compelled us to seek the refuge of the cart.

A royal welcome awaited us at Ellareddypett. Mr. Bursoji, the Avul Taluqudar (chief governor of the district), is a warm friend of Mr. Posnett's, so here in Mr. Bursoji's province everything was ours and the principal officials of the place, anxious to please their lord, treated us with the utmost kindness and consideration.

We were grateful for the courtesy which had placed at our disposal the best house in town, notwithstanding the readily overlooked discomfort of the small, dark rooms with walls dirty with the dirt of a dirty generation, and of the rickety wooden stairs of the step-ladder variety which led to a rough loft above and which swayed under our weight, threatening at every moment to precipitate us to the floor below.

As usual, we walked through the town in procession to let the people know we had come, and everywhere we were greeted most cordially. We saw several former patients, wives and children of rich Jain merchants, who loaded us with gifts of various foodstuffs and told our servants not to pay for supplies while in town, but to send to them for anything we wished.

The Jains, few in number, are the remnant of the Indian Buddhists, and their faces show clearly their Mongolian origin. They are extremists in the matter of protecting animal life. They cremate their dead on a stone carefully brushed, that no insect life may be unwittingly taken, and they have established in Bombay an asylum for the lower animal life, including fleas and other insects; there men receive a daily wage for allowing the fleas to feed on their blood.

It seemed incongruous for the mother of the family, dressed in costliest silks and velvets and loaded with jewels, to squat beside her tiny, smoky stone fireplace and cook the evening meal with her own hands. This is compulsory on account of strict religious rules in regard to the purity of food eaten. This same lady showed us with fond pride her bedroom, a closet-like apartment, with one small window—its only furniture a string cot and a tall brass stand holding a clay lamp. All around the wall on shelves were dozens of brass and silver-plated cups and mugs and vases, while from the ceiling hung suspended colored balls of tinsel like Christmas tree ornaments.

When bedtime came, I recalled one of little Eva Adkin's remarks. The mosquitoes had been unusually troublesome at Medak, and Eva inquired: "Mother, what is the use of mosquitoes?"

"I don't know, dear," replied her mother, "but everything God has placed on earth is of some use."

"I suppose," concluded Eva thoughtfully,

"when I go to heaven it wouldn't be polite to ask God about that."

My meditations at Ellareddypett were to the effect that I should risk the impropriety and seek a reason for the existence of the pests. When the torment from the vicious creatures became absolutely unendurable, we formed rolls from newspapers and, covering our heads with the sheet, pushed one end of the roll outside, making a passage for the air. When sleep overcame us, the rolls fell to the floor and we slept on unconscious of the vitiated air until the dawn found us gasping for breath and coolness.

A third of the inhabitants of Ellareddypett were afflicted with elephantiasis, that disease of slow and insidious development which gives to its victims monstrous limbs like the limbs of an elephant. The people thus affected appeared to think their misfortune a trivial matter, and laughingly showed us their misshapen limbs with the remark, "We want no medicine for it; it troubles us not at all."

On the last evening of our stay at his village, the Mahomedan Tahsildar of Ellareddypett sent us a sumptuous dinner and called a few hours later to say farewell. The old man is childless, but he accepts this greatest affliction with a philosophy worthy of imitation.

"I had children, boys and girls, but they are dead!" he sighed. *"Kismet!* We are taught not to grieve," and, touching his brow with his forefinger, he turned away with a patient smile.

For our protection on the road to our next stopping place, the Tahsildar sent with us a government *chaprassi.*

"What!" exclaimed the *chaprassi* in injured tones, when the Tahsildar admonished him to take good care of us. "Will I not protect the Mem Sahibs? Do I not wear this?" And he clapped his hand boastfully on his brass plate of office attached to the shabbiest of brown shoulder straps. The noble gallant proved his devotion by always being somewhere else when wanted and by valiantly hitting with his stick the small boys who came in innocent curiosity to gaze at the white ladies.

So, safe in the care of the doughty *chaprassi,* we passed through the old crumbling city gate and came immediately upon a holy well, a structure about twenty feet square by many more deep, with elaborately carved stone balconies. All around the inside were stone steps leading to the water, by which the worshiper goes down into the well and leaves it after his bath of purification to enter one of the near-by temples, each dedicated to a different god. After ringing a bell to call the attention of the god to his presence, the devotee places his offering at the altar and prostrates himself in prayer.

The idol in each temple is locked in a small room where only the privileged may enter, but we peeped through the chinks in one of the doors, and as our eyes became accustomed to the darkness we could see the gaudy, hideous thing in its gold and silver ornaments perched on its sacred chair, while the strong smell of incense reached our nostrils.

At Kaliampett, the officials of the village placed the new *dak* bungalow at our service and, like the Ellareddypett officials, did all they could to make our visit pleasant.

Chota hazrai was scarcely over next morning when Abbishakamma came running to say that in the night, at the very gates of the village, a leopard had injured a woman and that they were bringing her to us. The victim, a Lombardy (Indian gypsy) girl barely nineteen years of age, was terribly mutilated about the face and chest; blood dripped from the wounds; her face was convulsed with terror; and she constantly screamed, "*Yahdardai! Yahdardai!*" (Oh me! Oh me!)

The savage creature had struck her as she lay sleeping, her shrieks had awakened the rest, and their cries had driven it away. As it slunk off, however, it snatched from its mother's arms a boy three months old, and bore him away to the woods. The poor mother, they told me, refused to be comforted, and there was terrible confusion in the gypsy camp.

After dressing her wounds, we sent the girl away somewhat pacified, but, through the wilderness of bandages and strapping, there still came the low frightened moan, *"Yahdardai! Yahdardai!"*

Our next stopping place was on the homeward route at a large, clean village by the side of a clear lake, and we pitched our tent under a hospitably spreading tamarind tree. Then for several days we led a gypsy life in the jungle.

The cooking was done in a stone fireplace under a tree, and, in spite of the primitive conveniences, excellent meals were prepared. Though the eggs were strained through the cook's unwashed fingers and the dishes were dried on the duster, we were grateful that the eggs were not strained, as is sometimes the case, through the cook's sleeping-blanket, and that the dishes were not dried, as they frequently are, on the lamp cloth.

All day long people thronged to the tent, some for medicine, some to satisfy their curiosity.

On the first day came the important officials of

the village, who tried to sit on chairs in the English manner, but who continually forgot and restlessly curled their feet under them or drew their knees to their chins as they talked.

Then followed the villagers, each holding out a hand, with the laconic, *"Jerra soodoo!"* (Just see!) and when we asked them if they suffered pain, staring in surprise with the exclamation: "You have felt my pulse; you are a doctor; should you not know better than we?"

There were also the women who came timidly to the tent, now drawing near and now retreating, needing medicine but afraid to drink for fear of some evil result from the drugs of the "foreigner." One of them told us she feared to drink the medicine lest her babies be born white.

"Never mind!" I replied, "if your children are born white, put them out in the sun a little while; they will soon be black enough."

Several of the women hid the faces of the babies lest we should cast the "evil eye" upon them.

The usual number of questions were asked as to what we ate and how, why we came to India, what salary we received, how old we were, whether Miss Tombleson and I were sisters or merely of the same caste, where our husbands were, and other delicate and impersonal inquiries, till our brains and tongues wearied with the effort of making tactful and noncommittal answers.

Came also the hopeless cases that had tried everything else before risking treatment by the "white people."

And with them all those sufferers who greatly needed us and wanted us and for whose sake only we should gladly have come.

It was rather a shock to such faith as the people had in us when they learned that we could not give brains to an idiot girl nor arms to a babe born without those useful members, but, in spite of our glaring failures of this sort, they showed no lack of cordiality in their request that we come to their village once a week with medicines.

At the end of every day, after the crowds about the tent had gone to their homes for the evening meal, Miss Tombleson and I would have a short swim in the lake or, lounging on the steps of one of those ruined temples almost invariably found on the banks of Indian lakes, we would pass the time with song or story or silently watch the glorious color pageant in the western sky.

After dinner we would play chess in the light of the big lantern until roused from our absorption in the game by the tempting fragrance of hot chocolate and the voice of the boy over the steaming cups: "Missy ordering hot chocolate at bedtime; I bringing."

So our tour ended and we came back, half glad, half sorry, to the routine of life at Medak.

XVII

ON HORSEBACK AND OFF

OUR ponies were startled when, as we rode through Medak one evening, a man suddenly appeared in front of us sobbing and begging us to save the life of his daughter. We stopped to see what we could do, but always the same old story. The medicine of every *hakim* in the place had been tried, and we were called in when but a flicker of hope remained.

I saw that the little girl's life was nearly ended, but I gave her some medicine.

"I am your loving daughter, Doctor Mem Sahib!" she whispered, her thin hand weakly clasping mine. "You will cure me, won't you?" Then, after a brief silence, and shyly: "You have such beautiful dolls! If I had a doll, I think I should get well."

Hastening to the compound, I returned with a pretty English doll and, as the child clasped it in her arms, her smile was radiant.

"Now I shall get well very fast," she murmured and sank into the death stupor.

Two hours later when I called again, the loud wailing told its own story. The child spirit had gone home, and the doll still lay close against the quiet little bosom.

It was an interesting change from our usual twilight gallop on the ponies when Dadu Badsha lent us one of his elephants for a ride.

An elephant's back is as accommodating as a Broadway surface car—always room for one more—so eight of us, by the help of a ladder against the side of the kneeling elephant, and the supplementary aid of our "Padre Sahib's" strong right arm, mounted. Then, holding for dear life to the ropes that fastened the blankets securely in place, we waited until the changing slant of the broad back had become level before we breathed again. So, clinging fast to the ropes, we swung and lunged and swayed as the elephant ponderously made a circuit of the compound, and the anxious *mahout,* seated on the elephant's neck with his cruel-looking hook in hand, glanced round every little while to see if the laughing, careless riders behind him were safe.

"How terrible it would be if we should fall!" exclaimed Mrs. Adkin, taking a firmer grip on the rope.

"Don't worry, Mother!" said five-year-old Eric, reassuringly clasping his arms about his mother's waist. "You cannot fall for I will hold you very tightly!"

The sun was sinking to-day when we returned from our village visits, and we were somewhat alarmed for, in spite of the teachings of the Koran and the Vedas, many Mahomedan and Hindu peasants get drunk every evening at twilight, and the scenes in the village at that time are both pitiful and disgusting. It is not unusual to see a babe of four or five years reeling drunkenly from one to another of his drunken parents, who, laughing uproariously at the child's efforts to control his feet and tongue, ply him with more rice liquor or palm toddy until he drops helpless.

On the evening of which I write we urged our ponies to special haste and were glad when we found ourselves within the gates of the compound, for the feast of *Sankurathri* would soon begin.

To everyone who knows of the Hindu gods and the bestiality ascribed to most of them it will bring no surprise that the Hindus have an annual feast of several days when they give themselves entirely to the satisfaction of their lower natures, lying, thieving and otherwise wronging each other with impunity. On the last night, called *"Sankurathri,"* every Hindu may, without sin, commit adultery. From the compound we could plainly hear the drunken, discordant shouts and singing of the villagers, as they celebrated this abominable feast.

Not all the Hindu festivals are so abhorrent. The feast of Battakamma, part of the great feast of Dasara, for the worship of Sarasvathi, goddess of knowledge, has many beautiful and poetic features.

To celebrate Dasara, the princes and nobles give dinners to the people; everybody takes a holiday and wears new clothes; ancestors are worshiped; the soldier bows to his sword, the merchant to his pile of money, the farmer to his plow, and all other men to the implements of their various occupations. The streets are full of shouting, singing Hindus and of garlands, bouquets, and banks of flowers. Brahman schoolboys, decorated from head to foot with flowers and carrying wands and bows and arrows made of flowers, walk in procession through the town following their schoolmaster and stopping at the doors of houses where they are likely to receive a present. The Mission bungalows are always favored and before an interested audience they sing in loud, shrill tones various action-songs, until, notwithstanding the picturesque appearance of the chorus, the missionaries are compelled to preserve their ear-drums intact by giving a rupee to the joyous little bands, who *salaam* courteously and depart.

Nevertheless, even Dasara has its bitterness, for every man, no matter how poor, is compelled by public opinion, the merciless arbiter of India's fate, to celebrate properly the feast even though he sell his own child to obtain money so to do.

And there is another sort of cruelty. An important ceremony of the festival is the sacrifice of a goat. Part of the goat's tail is cut off and red pepper applied to the wound. In agony the poor creature violently shakes the stump, scattering blood on the bystanders, who eagerly rub their fingers in it and place the bloody fingers on their foreheads. Then, as the goat must die a sacrifice by the hand of man without the use of a knife, this "hand of man" drives a nail into each of the goat's eyes and ears and into every other orifice of the body, and finishes the sacrifice by literally tearing the tortured beast to pieces.

Knowing such things as this, do you wonder that my mind sometimes reverts to the frequently recurring statements in our popular Western journals, where we of the Occident are advised to learn humanity from the East Indian?

It is true that Hindus worship many varieties of dumb animals; it is true, they do not often kill them outright. They look on indifferently at a sick brute's hours or days of agony—hopeless agony preceding death—and nothing would shock the Indian more or cause his eyes to open wider in horror than the suggestion that he kill the creature instantly.

I love my Indian people, and I should like to concur in the optimistic opinion of them held by our journals at home, but I should indeed be a fatuous believer in the untrue to thus discredit the evidence of my own senses.

In extenuation, however, let me add that the barbarities practiced by the East Indian usually arise not from a malignant spirit, but from a childish lack of imagination or from an apathy born of the tropics.

In one of the *zenanas* I visited I saw a partridge in a cage so small that he could scarcely stretch his neck. The people told me they had caught two but one had died and this one was always pecking at the bars trying to free himself. At my request, they gave me the bird and, as I rode past a cornfield, I tossed the trembling captive from my hand and he fluttered joyously away into the corn.

One day I galloped past a group of men who stood about some object and from sheer curiosity I reined in my pony to see what was happening. One of the men had shot a flying fox through the wing and was holding it out in all its broad expanse while another man was arranging a camera for a photograph. The torn flesh dripped blood and at intervals of about ten seconds a bystander would strike with a stick the broken bone, for the pleasure of seeing the wounded creature shrink back in agony. Each time the act was followed by a loud laugh from everybody present. The stern lecture I administered seemed to shame the men, and they promised to take the photograph and set the animal free without further torture.

It is common in Bombay to load road carts so full that the bullocks are thrown up into the air from the burden.

Only by the utmost caution and strict supervision can a Western man keep his own dumb beasts from being starved by their caretakers, who ruthlessly steal their food and otherwise shamefully neglect them. Sister Adela Moss, one of our English ladies, riding in the bullock *tonga* with a driver who had newly come to the compound, saw him plunge an iron-pointed stick into the back of the bullock as he drove, and she instantly commanded him to throw away his weapon of torture. A moment later, she noticed blood trickling down the bullock's tail and, watching closely, she saw the driver bend his head and deliberately bite with his own teeth the beast's tail until it bled afresh.

Notwithstanding my constant horseback riding, I was thrown one day and at the same time had a snake adventure. It was on one of my visits to a far village. My pony was forcing his way through a dense undergrowth in the forest, when I heard a rustle, and an immense python wriggled from the bush straight for my horse's legs. The pony trembled violently. Realizing what would happen, and remembering an old bicycle trick of relaxing and letting myself fall easily, I dropped to the bushes just as the pony reared and jumped sidewise into a roadside pond of muddy water. The snake was so long that I nearly fell on its tail; but we all escaped unhurt —horse, snake, and woman. My hearty laugh as the ashen-faced *syce* helped me to my feet brought back the blood to his cheek, and without further adventure we proceeded on our way.

XVIII

THE JAHTRA

IF obstacles cause one to appreciate the goal, then surely we should have enjoyed the Jahtra. The Jahtra is a sort of Hindu county fair, where once a year the Hindus by thousands meet in a certain place and beseech the gods to give them children, or they make sacrifices as thank-offerings for children already granted.

Rising before dawn, we piled ourselves and a good supply of medicine into the *bandies* and started off. Now, one may cross the Manjery River only by boat or by way of the new dam built in connection with the Manjery Irrigation Project, which has proved an immeasurable blessing to the Medak District. This dam stretches from shore to shore, a mile of mud-covered, slippery stones forming a path some four feet wide, with water two or three inches deep dashing swiftly over it to a bed of boulders twenty feet below. You may imagine our procession: Miss Tombleson, Miss Wigfield and I in front, barefooted, with now and then a slip, a cry, and a regaining of our balance; the nurses and servants with luggage on their heads following; poor old Abbishakamma gray with fright, shrinking between two men and holding desperately to their arms; and before us and behind us a long unbroken line of Indians in gay holiday attire.

At the scene of the Jahtra itself not a tree was in sight, but boulders, boulders, boulders, covering the hills and causing us to make our way along the paths by jumping from rock to rock.

The smell of roasting flesh greeted us as we came upon a Hindu family who, with the help of two or three priests, were offering up a sheep in thanks for a chubby infant who rolled on the ground at his mother's feet. The sheep's head was roasting on the fire beside a black pot all marked with streaks of red and green and yellow and decorated with flowers, this pot holding the rice which would be eaten a little later at the feast. The father, who was skinning the sheep's body, was delighted to tell us all about the matter; how last year he had come to this place to pray for a boy and how this year he had brought the boy himself.

Almost immediately we came upon another scene still more impressive. In a little hollow of the rocks over a dirty pool of water presided a coarse-faced, outcaste priest. Whoever should bathe in this water and receive his blessing would be granted a child. And here they came, low caste and high, the eager faith of the high caste women causing them to forget, in their longing for domestic happiness, that the touch of the priest was defilement. They poured the filthy water over their bodies, and an old hag helped the priest to empty bowl after bowl of the water upon their heads. On the surface of the pool they placed flowers and the sacred *tulsi* plant; they marked the rocky sides of the pool with red and yellow, rubbed the yellow dye well into their own faces and hands, and the priest solemnly placed a red mark upon their foreheads. Then, shivering and dripping, they walked several times around the pool, placed a few *pice* in the hand of the priest, and departed for a continuation of the ceremony elsewhere. Following them, we came to a cave in the rocks where the priests had erected an "altar," and here the women received a garland and another blessing and went away hopeful. As we watched, Miss Wigfield's righteous indignation burst forth:

"Why do you deceive these poor women so? The great, true God alone can give them children."

And it rather took us aback when the priest replied—the women listening to every word:

"Of course, this is all of no use. We know the gods will not grant children because of this. We do it to fill our stomachs. It is but a few *pice* and the women wish to pay it."

And still, with his words in their ears, they allowed him to place the garlands about their necks and gladly put their *pice* into his hand.

All day long there were new scenes and fresh excitement; the bazaars were bright with cloths, foodstuffs, cheap jewelry and toys. A purple horse of most astounding anatomy inspired us to the paraphrase,

> We never saw a purple horse;
> We never want to see one;
> But this we'll tell you that, of course,
> We'd rather see than be one.

Performing bears and monkeys were put through their tricks; beggars showed their loathsome deformities; vile intoxicants were sold at every turn; young women and boys and hideous old witches wildly danced and shrieked, then trembling violently sank to the ground in a religious "trance."

What seemed in the eyes of the people the chief feature of the fair was a procession of some twenty *bandies,* filled with laughing youths, each *bandy* gay with paint and paper and tinsel, and drawn by a pair of bullocks decked out with bright streamers. All the long afternoon the *bandies* twined in and out among the rocks with never a pause, and always where they went the crowd was thickest.

Just back of our tent whirled and danced and chanted a low-browed *fakir,* nude but for a loin cloth, and with his hair hanging below his knees, each separate strand so matted with dirt and grease that it might have been a leathern thong. A mother brought her baby to be blessed and the *fakir* paused long enough in his violent exercises to pass a strand of his hair over the baby's face, to mutter a few words of blessing and receive his pay; and then continued in his untiring evolutions.

We were delighted to see at the Jahtra many old friends. Every little while, as we passed along on our sightseeing expedition, somebody would dash from the crowd and throw himself at our feet or upon our shoulders, and we would recognize a grateful patient or an equally grateful relative of a patient.

In the afternoon we dispensed medicines in the tent and though but few came to us, those few seemed impressed with Abbishakamma's story, told as only Abbishakamma can tell it, of heart-broken, childless Hannah and the little God-given Samuel.

XIX

RICE CHRISTIANS

FREQUENTLY in magazines and newspapers appear sarcastic comments on foreign mission work, which intimate that the converts to Christianity are merely "rice Christians," that is, men who accept Christianity for the worldly benefit they receive by so doing.

I admit that many of our converts began as "rice Christians," but the nature of the Hindu is all conservatism. When he has, for any reason, left a beaten path in life, the new path he has chosen soon becomes as dear to his nature as was the old, and it would require as enormous an effort to force him from it. From a "rice Christian" he becomes as true a follower of Christ as the majority of Westerners reared in the faith.

Rajannah, a high-caste Hindu without near relatives, had been deserted because of his helplessness due to complete cataract of both eyes. When he came a beggar to the compound, Dr. Watts, to whose position at Medak I succeeded, operated on his eyes and restored to him partial sight. Deeply grateful, he professed Christianity, and both Dr. Watts and Miss Wigfield took a warm interest in his spiritual development, which seemed very rapid. When the time came for him to be baptized, the ladies assured Mr. Posnett that Rajannah was very intelligent and understood perfectly what baptism meant. As the old man stood in church before the whole congregation, Mr. Posnett questioned him as he questions all converts:

"Rajannah, why have you become a Christian?"

"What could I do?" answered Rajannah. "I had no rice to fill my stomach, and I knew you would give me rice and work."

Months later he was able to pass more successfully an examination for baptism, and when he was too old and weak to do more than pull the *punkah,* we could daily hear his cracked voice singing hymns in tunes quite original, or preaching Christianity to the *dhirzi,* a high-caste Hindu who used to sit on our front veranda with his little hand-power sewing machine, and sew for us all day.

So Rajannah lived up to his light and, dying, told those who were with him that he should wake "in the Light of the Lord Jesus Christ."

Bordena Venkaiah shows another type of

Christian. Venkaiah had been notorious throughout the whole district for his brutality. He had beaten one wife to death and had drowned another in a well. Then he heard the teachings of Christianity, became converted, and was baptized. He asked us for one of our school-girls for a wife, but we feared to give her to him, thinking the old, evil temper might break out again. The girl herself, however, begged us to let her marry him, saying she trusted him. So we consented to the union and it proved a very happy one. Venkaiah was devoted to his girl wife, and his one wish was for a son to crown his joy. A daughter came and another, but no son. Through it all, Venkaiah remained patient and loving to his wife and little daughters, but his daily prayer was for a boy. Then the boy came. They named him Gabriel, and his father worshiped him. When the little son was baptized, Venkaiah adorned a young buffalo with garlands of flowers and, as a gift of gratitude, proudly led it up the aisle of the chapel to the altar.

Gabriel was about ten months old and very bonny, when his father came to our hospital and said: "I am called to the city and have left my wife and children alone in our village. If anything should happen to them, you will do what you can? They are my life!"

Scarcely two hours after his departure, the young wife came running with little Gabriel in her arms. He was in violent convulsions and just as she entered the hospital doors he died.

When Venkaiah learned the sad news, he was like a maniac, but, in all his raving, he never forgot that he was a son of God:

"O God, my Father, why have you slain my heart? O Gabriel, Gabriel!"

And so over and over again.

Several months later, when one of our missionaries passed the cemetery, she saw Venkaiah lying face downward on Baby Gabriel's grave, crying mournfully, "O Gabriel, my son, my son!"

Then another son came to him. When this child was born the young mother was alone in a distant village far from medical help, and, in giving life to the boy, lost her own. Venkaiah felt his wife's death keenly, but struggled on, fathering and mothering his little boy and girls. But the boy was always delicate and sickly and when one day Venkaiah brought him to our hospital the shadow of death already hovered over the sharpened features. After a few hours' lingering the baby died. As Venkaiah gazed on his dead child, his face was gray and drawn with his soul's agony, but this time there was no wild outburst of grief. Folding his arms, he said quietly:

"Now, all I have are in heaven but I am old and ready to go and I am glad they are all there waiting for me." Then, kneeling by the bedside, he prayed: "Now, O Lord, my Father, Thou hast all my treasures. Come again quickly and take me also to Thyself!"

Our old Kedari vies with Bordena Venkaiah in the manly strength of his Christianity. A high official of his village, father of five grown sons, and owner of many fields, Kedari became converted to Christianity and sacrificed for his belief his family, his property, his all. His own sons cursed and stoned him in the village streets; but, by patient endeavor, he at last won all his family to Christ, and every month thereafter Kedari, as his sons knelt beside him at the communion-rail, would smile proudly as he looked at them and then at his silver finger-ring which bore the Telugu inscription, "An elder in the Church of Christ!"

XX

GOD'S OUT-OF-DOORS

A CERTAIN queen in a castle was in trouble. This sounds like the beginning of a fairy tale, but it is a plain twentieth century fact, and the romance is somewhat modified by adding that the queen is an ancient dowager, mother of the late rajah, and the trouble was merely cataracts which she wished removed.

As the patient could not come to us and as there were no cases in hospital which we could not safely leave, Miss Posnett, Miss Harris and I started out to perform the operation at the queen's own castle in the village of Parpanapett on the outskirts of our district. We decided to make a regular medical tour, visiting Parpanapett in the natural order of the route.

Departing from the compound in the bullock *tonga,* we passed the potter just outside our gates squatting before his wheel which he swiftly turned, shaping with deft hands the clay pot before him. This scene brought to my mind, as it always did when I reflected on the souls of my dear Indian heathen, those comforting lines of Omar Khayyam's "Rubaiyat":

> Some there are who tell
> Of one who threatens he will toss to Hell
> The luckless pots he marr'd in making—Pish!
> He's a good fellow and 'twill all be well.

Two minutes later, we came to the massive gate in the old town wall of Medak and drove into the village, a typical village of India. The long, winding main street was lined with two rows of mud huts and crossed by narrow alleys, the uncovered sewage draining through street and alley. Brown monkeys jumped from house to house, the longest leap of a mother monkey disturbing not at all the baby clutching at her breast; and in the bazaar children, ponies, cows, buffaloes, donkeys, sheep, goats, dogs, cats, and hens commingled.

It was market-day and the merchants of the bazaar had spread their wares so far toward the middle of the street on both sides that only skilled guidance of the bullocks saved the careless vendors from ruin. Here and there a friend greeted us with a *salaam;* and gradually we wended our way around the hill with its old fort and temple and past the mosque where every morning at sunrise the Mahomedan priest cries from the minaret his "*Allah-il-Allah!*"—"God is God and Mahomet is his prophet! Come to prayer! Come to prayer! Come to prayer! Prayer is better than sleep!"

Then, out into the open country!

Far and wide extended plantations of cocoanut palms with an earthern vessel fastened to each to catch the juice which, when fermented, serves as toddy, the Indian beer. A lithe, brown coolie was taking down the filled vessels. To climb a tree, he leaned back against a rope fastened about his waist and the tree and rapidly worked his way up by means of his toes and knees.

In an adjoining field, swinging their trunks and lazily munching their hay, were Dadu Badsha's two tame elephants.

Beyond were castor-bean and mustard fields.

In front of their ancestral tombs, in the old Mahomedan burial ground, several Mahomedans prayed.

Here and there we saw the nest of the weaver bird swinging from a lofty branch. These nests are cleverly built and seem designed to protect the birds from snakes and other foes. A closely woven pyramid about a foot in length and depending by its apex from a branch swings loosely in the air. One side of the base forms a pouch where the bird may hatch her eggs, and the other side is lengthened into a cylinder leading from space into the nest, thus forming an opening which could be entered only by a winged creature of small size.

There were the usual fine old trees and the great heaps of boulders so common throughout this part of India; and always the green rice-fields, the white water-lilies, and the pink lotus flowers. We passed two or three droves of sturdy donkeys heavily laden; flocks of sheep and goats; springless wooden carts with their two rough wheels, each wheel a cross section of a tree trunk. Then we came to a lake of muddy water with the cattle rushing forward for a drink, and buffalo wallowing deep in the mire. A diver bird ran across our path; a ruined Hindu temple, relic of a thousand years ago, came to view; and, farther on, two or three bird scarers snug in their thatched towers carried out their unique, cobweb system. A rough straw shelter is built on a wooden platform raised high above the ground on four stout poles, smoothly polished to prevent snakes from climbing them. From this perch ropes extend in every direction, cobweb style, over the fields. Night and day a boy or girl sits on the perch to frighten away the thieving birds and beasts. In the daytime when

Toddy-drawing

birds only are the thieves, the child frightens them off by twitching the rope, and at night the little guardian of the hard-earned food shouts every now and then to keep the wild beasts away.

But we were on the road.

A chubby beggar boy ran behind the *tonga* slapping vigorously a well-rounded stomach, evidently trying to make us believe appearances deceitful.

A boy goatherd seated on a grassy knoll played on his pipe of reeds while he kept his goat from straying by clasping one of her hind feet firmly between the first and second toes of his right foot.

Down a steep incline our bullocks stumbled into the sandy bed of a river which in rainy weather is the largest river in this section of the country. Toddy shops, toddy shops everywhere! These are merely narrow roofs of thatch held up by poles and protecting the earthen pots of toddy and their keepers from the sun.

A car of Juggernaut—a Hindu temple on wheels—stood under its cover at the foot of the hill. Years ago, the Juggernaut cars used to play an earnest and terrible part in the religious life of Hindus throughout India. Frequently during a procession some fanatic would throw himself beneath the wheels of a car and be crushed to death. Though the cars still make occasional journeys, the English Government has forbidden the destruction of life, so the ceremony has lost to the Indian mind its chief attraction.

Farther on was a queer little stone monkey god, Hanamanthadu.

At Tardur, our first stopping place, the story had gone about that we had put a special drug in all the medicines to make those that should drink turn Christian, so only a few patients, and those timidly suspicious, came to us. We were, therefore, surprised when an old woman, her dark face all smiles and her tongue going at the rate of three hundred words a minute, rushed into the tent, and evidently overcome with joy or gratitude threw herself at our feet. By tactful questioning we learned that she was the mother of a Medak hospital patient whom a year previously we had cured of a serious illness.

"Where is your daughter?" we asked.

"She is coming but she is young and afraid. I will fetch her." So saying, the woman departed. An hour or two later she reappeared with the daughter, who shyly *salaamed.*

"I have brought her," said the mother triumphantly, "that she may kiss your feet. I have abused her all day that she has not come before.

Why are you afraid of the kind white ladies?" turning to the girl angrily.

"I am not afraid," replied the girl. "Why should I be afraid? Was I not in their hospital and did they not sit beside me and smile and hold my hand? No, I am not afraid," and, with eyes bulging from their sockets with terror, she dashed wildly through the tent door and away!

When an aged man started to drink the medicine we had given him, his equally aged spouse hastily turned his head toward a little stone goddess near by with the indignant remark, "How can you expect to be cured unless you turn your face toward the devil Poshamma and make *salaams?"* Miss Posnett, however, immediately took the medicine from him.

"No," she said, "this medicine is the gift of *Jesu Christu.* You must make *salaams* to no other god while drinking it."

The old man begged the medicine back and, gazing in terrified perplexity now at his wife and now at Miss Posnett, hastily gulped it down.

While in Tardur, we examined our Christian school, composed of a dozen tots, true village children, who stood in a neat row and answered bravely—all but one. She, a girl of four years, seemed very bashful, restless and ill at ease, constantly getting out of line and hiding behind her elder sister, a sedate motherly child of seven, who as constantly pulled her back. Suddenly, in one of her dives behind her sister, the baby divested herself of her one garment, a diminutive red *sari*, and stood forth quite naked and smiling serenely, her self-consciousness completely gone with her unaccustomed garb. All of us except the sister of the youthful Eve laughed heartily. She—poor child!—shocked to the core of her being, hastily retreated with the culprit, who soon reappeared with the offending garment once more draped about her plump figure.

Another move and we came to the village of Parpanapett, where our blind queen awaited us. There are, I feel sure, few villages in India lovelier than Parpanapett. It lies near a wide blue lake with rocky banks, the stone towers and high walls of the palace fortress and the rajah's garden, a paradise of bloom, forming a picturesque background.

When we called on Her Highness she graciously invited us to inspect the palace and, as her blindness prevented her from accompanying us, she sent one of her adopted sons instead. It was beautiful to see the reverence of these tall men for the frail old lady who has adopted them to fill, in some measure, the place of her dead son. Since the Rajah's death the palace has been given over to bats and other vermin. Only the *zenana* portion is inhabited, and we wandered through one desolate room after another; saw the exquisitely carved but worm-eaten chairs and tables, bed frames, and even an English bookcase; groped our way up the narrow stone staircases; smashed our topees in the low doorways, and finally emerged into the tower, where we had an extensive view of the country.

After the Parpanapett Rajah had died a cattle plague descended upon the village. You may not see the connection, but the villagers of Parpanapett saw it clearly enough and, dressing up a dummy to represent the dead Rajah, they daily sacrificed large numbers of sheep and goats before him to satisfy his angry spirit.

Our superintendent had joined us and in the evening after the medical day was over a religious meeting was held.

Some years before, our evangelist who had tried to preach Christianity in this village had been cruelly persecuted but by patience and courage had won the day and now his persecutors had come to be baptized. It was one of the most solemn and touching ceremonies I had ever witnessed.

The gray-haired men, gathered courageously together, asked earnestly and intelligently about their duties as Christians, and listened carefully while Mr. Posnett explained to them how serious was the step they were taking.

"We are brothers in Christ," impressively said their chief, the erstwhile leader of the persecution. "If we stand side by side and help each other to be strong, how can hatred or persecution matter to us?"

"And you must try to bring your children to the feet of Christ," said Mr. Posnett.

"Ha!" smiled one old man, "if the father be a Christian will the son dare be aught else?"

The Lombardies, who had their camp near ours, were a source of never-failing interest to us, a multiplicity of pariah dogs helping them to keep up one continuous performance in motion and commotion.

Young Lombardies are usually handsome and well developed. The dress of the women is composed of bits of cloth of every variety of color, sewed together after the manner and with the effect of a "crazy quilt," pieces of looking-glass and mica glistening from every part of their dress, while their large, coarse ornaments of iron, brass, bone, wood and precious metal make their every movement a loud jingling clank. Lombardy girls must have completed their entire costume—no easy task—before they are married, and, if you have ever seen the costume, you cannot wonder that they rarely attempt a second. The rags and tatters to which a dress is reduced as its wearer approaches middle life merely add to the attractiveness.

The gypsy folk are as shy as wood birds. Only death staring them directly in the face would coax them within the doors of a hospital. If they wish our medical treatment they make their home under a near-by tree, while we visit them there and minister to their needs. They are an industrious people. You never see a Lombardy sitting in the sun with listless hands, stopping to gossip for an hour at a village door, or begging for help. The tall, full figures are alive with energy and independence. As a Lombardy woman walks through the streets, a great bundle of sticks is on her head and in her hands is sewing work on which she is busily engaged. It is not surprising, then, that the Lombardies are rarely poor. Almost every family owns large herds of cattle.

Each year on one of their feast days, the Lombardy women come around to the bungalows and dance the famous "Lombardy dance," rising, bowing, bending sidewise and backward, squatting, swaying, all with admirable grace and rhythm; wizened, gray-haired women joining hands with handsome young girls and round-limbed children.

At bedtime every night on this tour to Parpanapett we had our cots pulled out under the trees and, as we sank to sleep, we drowsily watched the glare of the camp fire on the dark faces surrounding it, for in the evening half the village comes to gossip with our people.

So, picknicking outdoors for all our meals, and sleeping under the trees, with the Southern Cross blinking at us from the horizon, we traveled slowly homeward.

As we neared Medak, we passed the Indian mail-carrier. Resting on his shoulder was a strong, pointed stick on which his bag of mail was slung; at the end of the stick a cluster of little bells jingled musically as he trotted along at a swift, steady pace, while immediately behind him at the same pace ran his guard with drawn sword in hand.

XXI

OFF TO KASHMIR

THE famed Vale of Kashmir was our goal one year for the May rest, and the five English ladies and I went there together. At one of the stations where we made a long stop we had an opportunity to observe the details of a Mahomedan prayer. The bearded old man spread his rug before him, and, facing Mecca, began, in the light of the dying sun, his prayer to Allah. He touched his face rapidly here and there, now in front of the ears, now behind them; placed his clasped hands together; made a low obeisance, touching his forehead to the ground several times; stood or sat with hands on knees in the attitude of meditation; and so on through the whole time. Somebody came up and conversed with him; but the interruption seemed a matter of small moment. After a leisurely chat, he continued his prayer as before. Then he rolled up his rug, tucked it under his arm, and walked slowly away. Noticing the time, I found that the prayer itself, not counting the interruptions, had taken just nine minutes.

Three or four alligators sprawled on a sandy island in the almost dry river bed beneath the bridge over which our train passed.

A herd of wild deer gazed innocently at us from a wood near the track, then turned and bounded swiftly into the brush.

Grazing peacefully in a green field by the track was a herd of the small, hump-shouldered Indian cattle, with deer-like faces, resembling our Jerseys at home; the picturesque boy cowherd in loin-cloth and turban shaded his eyes with his hand as he gazed at the passing train.

In purple pajamas and red *chuddah*, an elderly woman bent low over something she was gathering in a near-by field. She did not look up as the train passed. The signs of the times were naught to her!

A young woman, clad in nothing but a loose red cloth fastened about her loins, balanced on her head the family water jar, her slim body swaying gracefully as she walked swiftly across the fields.

A jackal trotted leisurely over the plain, turned to look at the train rushing toward him, and scampered away with curious, sidewise leaps.

Up and down one of the platforms walked a group of Parsees. The gentleman of the party, in English dress except for his black, scuttle hat,

Swing bridge of Kashmir

Snake charmers and jugglers

led by the hand a little girl whose rich, olive complexion and dark, liquid eyes, and the green gauze veil draped artistically about her head and shoulders, seemed altogether out of keeping with the white English frock, the long, white pantalettes and the black shoes and stockings which formed the rest of her costume. The Parsee ladies wore soft silk *saris* of a delicate tint, with narrow, richly embroidered velvet border. The elder woman had the usual white cloth bound tightly about her head, this indicating that the wearer was married.

A herd of slate-gray, sleepy-eyed buffalo, with horns three or four feet long standing out at right angles from their heads, trailed past.

Then we were in the Punjaub, and we frequently saw a camel on the *maidan*, or an elephant trudging along the road with slow, majestic tread.

The people of the North, whose diet is wheat and pulse instead of rice, showed the effect of this better nourishment and of their colder, dryer climate in their fine physique and pride of carriage, as compared with our people on the Southern plains.

Lahore, *Kim's* city! And there were little Kims everywhere about the streets. Our guide showed us the points of interest, among them *Zam-*

Zammah, Kim's big gun, which stood close to the Museum. We pictured little *Kim* hurling abuse down upon his playmates from the top of the huge cannon; and we turned to the Museum where the simple, mild old Lama found a sympathetic soul in the keeper of the "Wonder House"; but the doors were locked and our train soon due, so we did not go inside.

The last railway station on the way to Kashmir is Rawal Pindi, and from there you have still before you one hundred miles of mountain road along the River Jhelum before you reach the Valley, rejoicing in a temperate climate at the height of fifty-five hundred feet above the sea.

Arranging for our baggage to follow us, we made the journey over the mountains in carriages.

After two years on the hot plains, it was bliss to draw deep into the lungs the cool, life-giving air of the pines; to see the white clematis and hawthorn, the pink roses and sunny buttercups on every hand, the shy wild strawberries hiding their crimson among the grass by the way, and the dainty maidenhair fern covering the rocks in a lavish expenditure of riches. When the delicate fragrance of the wood violet greeted our nostrils, we were tempted from our carriages for a short rest on the mossy banks beside the road where the blue darlings were thickly scattered. Suddenly a patch of snow in the brush caught our eye, and we promptly indulged in an old-fashioned snowball fight. It was great fun, but our drivers were so frightened that their teeth chattered. They thought we were in earnest, and begged us to make peace with each other, until, in mercy to the poor fellows, we gave it up, and our laughter, as we climbed back into the carriages, seemed greatly to relieve their minds.

We stopped for the night and for meals at the well-equipped *dak* bungalows all along the route, where frequently we met pleasant fellow-travelers.

For four days we traveled through that magnificent mountain scenery where *Feramorz* won the heart of his *Lalla Rookh*.

Hundreds of feet below our pathway the Jhelum River brawled and tumbled. Far above us the snow mountains stood out against the sky hemming us in on every side until, as we gazed at them, we felt chilled and awed by their solemnity, but the golden bird-songs from the meadow told us of warm, throbbing life, and we turned again to the flowers and the butterflies.

An immense drove of camels coming down from the Khyber Pass met us one day. Some of the camels were wee babies and the funniest, fuzziest little fellows imaginable.

There also met us a party of big, rough-looking Afghanese, with peaked turbans and long coats, and several groups of those polyandrous mountain people in whose family the woman reigns supreme, like a queen bee, over her half-dozen husbands.

We were lunching in a grove on the way when a pack of great, white pariah dogs rushed toward us. Leaping, growling, fighting, they savagely snatched the bread from our hands and from the basket beside us. We did not argue the point, but hastily left the scene and the remnants of the lunch.

Toward the end of our route, the long-haired Kashmir goats appeared, balancing on sharp pinnacles or jumping fearlessly from crag to crag.

On the mountains along the way we frequently saw signs of human life, bazaars to tempt the traveler, villages with the ever-present fort, and old mosques and temples which I could with pleasure have examined more closely.

So we rode on until the mountain pass gave way to the broad and verdant plain, and we left our carriages for the *dhunga* which our Srinagar hostess had sent to meet us.

Kashmiri women

A *dhunga* is a large, flat boat of old walnut wood beautifully hand carved in all sorts of intricate designs, with roof and sides of matting. Sometimes the boatman and his family put themselves into harness and trudge along the bank, dragging the *dhunga* by ropes; sometimes they all get inside and paddle it slowly along by means of a peculiar oar—a long handle and a heart-shaped blade.

Within the *dhunga* there is every comfort for the traveler, a tiny suite of rooms, dining room, bedroom, dressing room and bathroom, and an open space in front for a sitting room. Each of these rooms is shut off by matting curtains, and back of all the boatman and his family live.

This was our first view of the natives of Kashmir, people who well deserve their reputation for physical beauty. The large, well-knit figure, the clear, olive skin, with damask rose showing on the cheeks, and the handsome Jewish features seem to speak of superiority in every way; but, alas! they have been for so many centuries a subject people, that now, mentally and morally, they have only a quickness at repartee and a cringing good nature to recommend them.

The costume of both men and women consists of a number of loose, long coats with full sleeves. In cool weather they pile on extra coats and help the warming process by tying about the waist under their clothing a *kangra* (a clay, basket-covered pot) full of live coals.

The women and girls wear a great deal of cheap, showy jewelry, and arrange their hair in numberless thin plaits, tying all the plaits together at the end with a narrow, black ribbon which hangs almost to the ground.

The Kashmiris have the praiseworthy custom of washing themselves and their clothes occasionally—once every six months by strict compulsion of the Government.

Peasants of Kashmir address every white person as *"Huzoor"* (Your Highness). This was a custom unknown to me when I asked our boatman what I should call the sweeper or refuse-carrier, one of a class which, throughout India, are outcast of the outcastes.

"Huzoor?" inquired the boatman, meaning, "I beg your pardon, what did you say?"

"Oh, *'Huzoor,'* is it?" I said, quite satisfied, and for many days I continued, in my ignorance, to address the poor menial as "Your Highness."

The *dhunga* bore us along down the river, out through Wular Lake, the largest lake in India, and wonderfully beautiful in its perfect tranquillity with the brilliant reflections of the snow mountains in its depths, on to the river again, and so to Srinagar, where we found our houseboat.

Place the rooms of a summer cottage end to end, mount them on a carved walnut barge, place a veranda on top of all, and you have a Kashmir houseboat.

Most of the European visitors in Srinagar live in such houseboats and move about the city—a real Venice of the Orient—by means of graceful little *shikarras* (native rowboats).

Obtaining the necessary permit from the Resident to remain in Kashmir for a time, we surrendered ourselves to a life of "sweet do-nothingness" in that love-haunted and loveliest of vales,

> With its roses the brightest that earth ever gave,
> Its temples, and grottos, and fountains as clear
> As the love-lighted eyes that hang over their wave.

XXII

SUMMER SIGHTSEEING

AGAIN our train sped toward Medak and work and reality!

Our first stop on the homeward journey was at Amritsar, the "City of the Sikhs."

Before we entered the Golden Temple, cloth shoes were tied over the "unholy" leather of our footgear, and in these we "galumphed" about and saw the "sights."

Day and night, one priest or another drones out the sacred words of the "Granth" before an ever-burning lamp. It was a peaceful sight—the disciples, the youth of the Sikhs, seated about the old, white-haired priest, listening to the words as they fell from his lips, while the temple doves helped themselves to the wheat spread out on the floor as an offering to the gods, or in friendly fashion took the grains from our hands.

The Sikh costume seemed to me the most manly in India. The lower garment made of thin, white cloth in the form of trousers, short and full and falling to the knee, impressed me more favorably than the effeminate flowing *dhoti* or the long skirt. The Sikhs never cut the hair or beard, and usually wear about the turban the *chekram,* a steel ring or quoit, thin, flat, and razor-sharp, which they can throw, when occasion requires, with deadly skill.

A good-natured *ayah* in charge of the waiting-room at the Amritsar station brought us our tea. As she placed the tray with its tempting contents before us, she wiped her well-oiled hair and sweat-bedewed face with her broad, brown hands, exclaiming, "Very hot, Missy Sahib!" Then, before we could prevent her, she seized a slice of the delicately browned toast and, crushing it in her hand, held it out toward Miss Richardson, asking innocently: "You liking toast, Missy Sahib? You eating toast?"

"Well, not now," replied Miss Richardson, whom fever and the intense heat had left with little appetite in any event, and, turning white about the mouth, she suddenly left the room, while the *ayah* looked after her in amazement.

A few stations farther on Miss Richardson and I left the rest of our party and went somewhat out of our way to visit Lucknow and Cawnpore, the cities that suffered most in the great Mutiny of 1857.

At Lucknow we engaged an *ekka* to take us to the ruined Residency.

An *ekka* is the queerest little cart imaginable —a small wooden platform on two wheels, with a canopy for a top and drawn by a single horse. On the wooden platform one must sit cross-legged like the Indians, or let the feet hang down over the wheel, as the English usually prefer to do. So, holding our skirts away from the wheels as best we might, we rattled and jounced merrily along to our destination.

The buildings are a mass of vine-covered ruins full of great holes and gashes where for five, long, heart-breaking months the "millions of musket bullets and thousands of cannon balls" poured in unceasingly.

We climbed to the "topmost roof" where all through the siege the "banner of England blew." The flag of England still flies on the mended flag-staff. As fast as worn out, it is replaced by a new one, and always floats proudly over the ruins below, the only flag of the British Empire that is never lowered.

We heard again the story of Jessie Brown, the Scotch girl, how she had dreamed she heard the pibroch and prophesied the immediate coming of Sir Colin Campbell and his Highlanders, and how that very day the pibrochs really sounded and a loud cheer from the earthworks told that Sir Colin had arrived.

We saw the gap in the wall caused by the bomb which ended the life of the brave and beloved commander, Sir Henry Lawrence, and outside the great white marble cross that marks his resting-place. On it are inscribed the words which he himself requested for his epitaph:

> Here lies Henry Lawrence who tried to do his duty.
> May the Lord have mercy on his soul!
> Born 28th of June, 1806. Died 4th of July, 1857.

Leaving the Residency, we visited several other buildings, all vibrant with memories of the siege; looked with interest on the Bailey Guard Gate held so bravely by Lieutenant Aitken and his loyal Sepoys; gave a few coins to the tottering old Indian *bhisti* (water-carrier) who had been the *bhisti* at the time of the siege, and dashed away to the station with barely time to catch the train for Cawnpore.

On reaching Cawnpore, we lost no time in driving out to see the "Angel."

Poor Cawnpore of tragic memory! A place of memories only, the smiling green of to-day hiding all traces of the bloody, pitiless carnage enacted there fifty years ago!

We strolled leisurely about, inspecting Marochetti's beautiful white marble statue which stands above the well where the bodies of the British women and children were thrown. In front of a cross the angel stands, looking downward, her arms folded on her breast and the palm branch of martyrdom in each hand, the tender peace of her face seeming to banish all hatred against the perpetrators of the deed which she commemorates. On the pedestal an inscription reads:

> Sacred to the perpetual memory of the great company of Christian people, chiefly women and children, who, near this spot, were cruelly massacred by the followers of the rebel Nana Doondoo Panth, of Bithoor, and cast, the dying and the dead, into the well below, on the 15th day of July, 1857.

An octagonal Gothic screen surrounds the statue, and over the arched entrance are the words:

> "These are they which came out of great tribulation."

Outside this screen is a circle of cypress trees, and the whole is in a wide park rich with verdure.

We were charmed and awed by the beauty and solemnity of it all, but the intense heat and glare of noonday soon made us long for the shelter of our carriage. Our driver, being an Indian, was, by the city laws, forbidden the grounds, so we had told him to wait for us at the gate. We walked quickly back to the gate, but the carriage had vanished. Calling loudly, we waited. Minute after minute went by, but there was no sign of the driver or his vehicle, and we never again saw either. Not knowing which way to turn, for we had been too busy with the sights of the city to notice our route from the station, we asked several of the passers-by where we might find a carriage, but all replied in the same apathetic voice and with a shrug of stupid indifference, "A carriage? How should I know where you can get a carriage?" Then we asked: "Where is the railway station?" And the answer came with the same shrug: "The railway station? How should I know where it is?" So we turned back into the garden to wait, hoping our driver might return. In circling about we lost our bearings, and, try as we might, could not find the entrance again. After a half-hour of fruitless search I spied a drain-hole under the fence. It was dry and choked with dead leaves, but, by pushing the leaves away, there was room for a person to squeeze through, and, lying flat on our faces, we did so. Rising and brushing the dust from our clothes, we found ourselves in a strange street, and looked up and down in vain for a white face.

It was the hottest part of the day in the hottest month of the year in the hottest city of all hot India. Miss Richardson's eyes and cheeks were flushed with fever, and when we espied a wayside pump we almost ran toward it. A copious draught of water seemed not to allay in the least our thirst. Time and again we left the pump only to return to it before we had gone a hundred yards away, drinking deeply each time, until I felt quite prepared for the old Chinese form of execution. (Man filled with water—board across stomach—two other men jumping on board—result evident!) But something had to be done beyond the drinking of water unless we wished to perish with sunstroke.

"Ah!" I exclaimed suddenly, "there is a chimney and smoke. That means a factory, and a factory means a white man. Ship ahoy!" and we hurried toward the blessed smokestack, my chest swelling with pride at my *Sherlock Holmes* deduction. Arrived at the smokestack, we found it surrounded by a high board fence and on the gate in large black letters, "No Admittance." Much we cared for signs and symbols just then. We pushed the gate open with bold hand and marched in.

"*Sahib hai?*" (Is the master in?), I asked of an astonished Indian.

"*Hai*" (He is in) was the laconic response.

"We would see him." So we were led into a large, comfortable-looking office, where at the desk sat a middle-aged English gentleman with a kindly face. Two hours under the fierce noon-day sun had quite upset my nerves, and I could have wept for joy on the man's neck, but, fortunately for him, restrained myself. He heard our story, immediately ordered iced water for us, and sent for a carriage. Conversing pleasantly under the cool *punkah,* we drank the delicious water, and by the time our carriage arrived felt quite refreshed. As we rode along in its grateful shelter, we admitted that we had for once known the full force of Tennyson's "heat like the mouth of a hell."

The thought of anything except the open air on such a day was intolerable, so we continued our sight-seeing.

At the ghat, where the treacherous river massacre took place, a memorial temple is in charge of an old Indian who receives a pension from the British Government. He said he had witnessed the whole tragedy, and told us of that terrible day on the river. With tears streaming down his face he exclaimed: "It was not the Sahibs nor the Mem Sahibs, but the *baba log* (children).

Oh, the *baba log!* I could not bear it!" And he hid his wrinkled old face in his hands.

A handsome memorial church stands over the site of the pitiful little fort where for three weeks, in a temperature ranging from 130 to 140 degrees Fahrenheit all day, three hundred starving, poorly armed British men, fighting with the mad courage of desperation, the sight of their helpless wives and little ones goading them on, kept at bay more than three thousand Sepoys, well fed, having abundant ammunition, and fighting at two or three hundred yards' distance from behind bullet-proof defenses.

In this memorial church we saw the colored sketch, made by an English artist a few days after the tragedy, of the room in the Bibi Ghar where the traitorous miscreant, Nana Sahib, caused the slaughter of the women and children. Clotted blood lay deep on the floor; saber-cuts showed low down on the walls; bloody finger-stains were everywhere; the children's quaint, old-fashioned bonnets, shoes and socks, blood-stained and torn, mingled with broken combs and toys, torn pages from books, and strands of hair. All the signs of that fearful confusion were depicted, and brought the scene so vividly before us that we felt sick and faint with horror.

At the station dinner we became engaged in

conversation with an elderly man who had been a soldier under Havelock and had seen the dreadful room in Bibi Ghar shortly after the massacre. He had a genial smile and a pleasant, courtly manner for us, but he seemed unable to address the Indian waiters in anything but harsh, peremptory tones. As he spoke of the Cawnpore events of '57, his eyes flashed hatred and he seemed as bitter about the Mutiny as if it had occurred last week.

"The dogs! The devils! The lying, thieving rats! I hate every one of them! I'll never forgive them! Don't you trust them! They'll do you every time."

The shadow of the Peace Angel's wings had not fallen across his wounded spirit.

From the day's stifling heat, the temperature had dropped to a delightful coolness, and after dinner we started out for a walk. The streets were full of soldiers, for a large British fort is at Cawnpore. English "Tommies" swung jauntily along, with tiny, round caps over their ears; great, brawny Highlanders strolled by in short trousers of plaid and the bonnet of the Scot; and now and then a gaily dressed British officer dashed past us on a handsome, well-groomed horse. It was fascinating, the city with its brilliant lights and busy life; and still more fascinating was the sudden change to the wide fields and quiet roads of the country, where the gentle rustle of the trees and the occasional soft chirp of a restless bird were all that broke the silence of the calm and shadow-subdued moonlight.

The ambient air with Unseen Things was stirred,
And the low music of the moving trees
Sang to the heart. The penetrating stars
And the majestic mistress of the night—
Fair, silver-sandaled moon—on her slow way
Across the spacious sky looked down between
The boughs that parted to the passing breeze,
Perfumed with breath of blossom and of rose,
Of aloe and acacia trees in bloom,
And all the pungent odors of the night.

XXIII

WOMEN OF INDIA

THE echoes of the Western slogan, "Votes for Women!" have not reached India.

A middle-aged woman came to our hospital bruised and bleeding from a beating she had received at the hands of her husband. She stated simply the cause of her wounds and asked medicine for them, while her husband, apparently unashamed, stood beside her, joining her in the request for "good medicine." When I took her into another room to apply the dressing, I asked indignantly: "Do you Indian women not feel bitterly humiliated and resentful when your husbands beat you thus?"

The woman gazed at me in surprise.

"Why, certainly not," she replied. "How else should we learn wisdom?"

No such reactionary spirit imbued the girl of Nandagaon, a Christian woman whose case was tried at court because she had deserted her husband and two-months-old baby. As we were touring at Nandagaon at the time of her trial, the *patel* invited us to be present.

Under a huge banyan tree the villagers had gathered, the judge, with the other chief officials, sitting on a bench, where we were asked to join them.

The prisoner, a pretty girl of sixteen, who had been brought in from the fields to meet her accusers, stood in the center of the group, her sickle in her hand and her red *sari* girt tightly around her shapely thighs.

"Let the prisoner speak!" shouted the judge, and everybody was silent, while the girl, throwing back her proud little head, made her plea in a clear, defiant voice.

"My husband and I became Christians. Then all the village people taunted me with cruel words. When I went to the village well for water, the other women pushed me away, crying: 'Don't touch our well! Don't come near our houses!' When I took my baby into the street they cried: 'You have brought the curses of the gods on the head of your son. Don't let your foul shadow rest on us! You are defiled!' I told my husband. He said: 'Heed them not! Bear it patiently!' Could I bear it? Could I? No. I begged my husband to take me to some village where there were other Christians, but he said he could not leave his work here. The women's curses rang day and night in my ears till they set my heart on fire. I could not bear it. I ran away."

The girl stopped, and a clamor of voices broke forth. Discipline there was none. Now and then could be heard the judge's voice: "Wait! Wait! Let me speak!" But nobody paid the least attention until each man had decided in his own mind and had informed his neighbors what he thought should be done in the case. When at last the loud shouts had died to murmurs, the judge spoke:

"Your husband, at the advice and with the help of the kind English people, will settle in another town among Christians. Will you go back to him?"

"If I can go back and be told that I have done no wrong, yes. Otherwise——" and a defiant gesture ended her sentence.

"But your husband will have to beat you a little that you may not do this wrong again," said the judge.

"Then no!" shouted the girl. "I will not go back!"

"Well, well," broke in the husband mildly, "we could perhaps let the beating go this time. The babe needs his mother's care. Come home, woman"—he seized his wife's hand—"and I promise not to beat you."

So they walked off together, and the court adjourned.

The almost complete ignorance of the Indian woman enslaves her to the men of her family.

Mr. Posnett called one day on a high-caste Hindu prince, and, while they talked together, the princess, his wife, entered the room. Placing on the floor a basin of water she had brought, she knelt down and washed her husband's feet. When she had finished, she raised the basin to her lips and drank some of the water. Throughout the whole ceremony the husband seemed utterly unconcerned. When asked the meaning of the act, he answered simply, "That? Oh, she does that every day. For a devout and faithful Hindu wife it is one road to paradise."

It was in the cool of sunset when we led the mild-faced wife of a Mahomedan official of Medak up to the flat roof of the hospital to enjoy the lake breezes.

"Ah!" she exclaimed, gazing with wondering delight on the scene about her, "the only outdoor air I get is in our own courtyard. I remember the trees of my childhood home, but these I have never seen before, nor this lake, though for many years I have lived within a few rods of them. You English ladies should be very grateful for your liberty. Even when we go abroad into the streets our men carry us about like birds in a cage, only they put a curtain over the cage."

Hamed, an Arab boy of eight years, with pleading eyes and girlish features, had been for two years unable to walk owing to an injury of his leg. His mother, carrying him on her hip, brought him to our hospital, and after an operation and weeks of treatment, he left us proudly showing us how easily he could run down the steps.

A few days later his mother came to the dispensary door, and I immediately asked, "How is Hamed?"

"Oh," she replied, "the darling boy is well, quite well, and runs about like other children. This noon I did not prepare his dinner soon enough to suit him and he chased me all about the house, beating me with a big stick. See!" and she showed me great blue and bleeding welts on her arms and legs, "Hamed made these, and for these I have now come to get soothing medicine."

In the Orient, masculine supremacy runs rife through the veins of even the infant man-child. A woman came into the dispensary leading by the hand a boy of perhaps five years. When I had heard her story and offered her medicine to drink she shrank back, but her small son, in the most imperious manner possible, pulled at her *sari,* exclaiming, "What! You won't drink! Sit down here at once and drink the medicine as the Doctor Mem Sahib tells you to!" As she obediently squatted down, he stood beside her with uplifted hand and threatened, "Hi, hi! Drink, I tell you!" until every drop was drained.

From this you will see that the author of an article in a leading magazine at home had seen little of Indian home life when he wrote that the child who could say "Shut up!" to its parents had never been "conceived or conceived of" in India. Not only "Shut up!" but the foulest language and emphasizing kicks and blows from child to both mother and father are everyday occurrences. On the whole, I cannot imagine any children less controlled than those of India. After the children are grown, however, there are an attractive reverence and dutifulness to the parents unusual in the West. To marry against a parent's command, to resent physical punishment, even though the receiver far exceed the giver in size, or to grumble against the burden of an aged and childish parent, would be, I should say, quite foreign to the East Indian.

The ignorance of the Indian woman also makes her childlike in many ways. A doll is caressed as warmly by the mother of several children as if one of her own babies were in her arms, and in many an Indian home, Mahomedan or Hindu, you will find the grown women playing happily with toy furniture or toy dishes.

We were frequently invited to a doll's wedding. At one we attended, the small boy of the house was espoused to the doll-bride with all the ceremonies and general festivities of a real wedding. A great feast was given and large sums of money were spent. When we asked to see the bride, the mistress of the house remonstrated with shocked face. "Why, don't you know that the bride is in *gosha* and must look on no face but that of her husband?" We told her she could grant us our wish by telling the doll-bride to keep her eyes down, so she smilingly led us into an inner apartment.

On a small dais, a bit of cloth shaped somewhat like a woman had been placed in a sitting posture. It was dressed in the correct bridal costume—magenta *chuddah,* crimson velvet pajamas, and green and yellow silk coat. In the center of what purported to be its face, a loop of thread held a tiny brass nose-ring; and its neck and arms and feet were hung with tiny jewels.

Among the many unhappy Mahomedan wives was one who came to our hospital begging treatment for an acute earache which had kept her awake for three nights. When I suggested that she stay in hospital and have the ear properly treated, she replied: "I will come again, but I cannot stay now. I have given my husband no children, so he is marrying another woman. He brings her home to-day, and I must go and make the house ready and prepare the wedding feast."

It is surprising, though, in what harmony these co-wives often live. In a case in the village a second wife had a very bad time after childbirth, and her most tender, devoted nurse was the first wife who had been discarded for the usual reason—lack of children. Again, when a slave girl, one of our patients in the village, bore her master a son and nearly died in convulsions, the master's wife was a mother to her throughout. Frequently, when you ask a woman carrying a child on her hip, "Is this your own child?" she replies: "No, it is the child of my husband's other wife, but I love it as my own."

Ratnamma, a young Brahman woman, was a patient in our hospital when I first came to Medak. One night she smiled at me so brightly that I said to an interpreter: "Tell her that her face is full of sunshine."

"Why not?" responded Ratnamma. "Great joy has come to me to-day." Then, yielding to her quiet urging, I sat beside her on her bed, and—a nurse interpreting her words to me—heard her story, the first part of which was already familiar to me.

At seventeen years of age she had given birth to the bonny boy who, as she told her tale, lay asleep in her arms. When the baby came the ignorant midwife had injured Ratnamma so that her husband refused to live with her, and, as is the custom in Hindu life, cast her out from his home. As Ratnamma's family was rich and noble, she did not suffer privation, but the reproaches heaped upon her, as upon all husbandless women of India, made her life miserable. Then came a message from her husband:

"I shall soon wed another woman, and when our son shall be weaned I shall take him from you."

Then was Ratnamma panic-stricken. As no *hakim* could help her, she turned in despair and with scant faith to the despised Christians. Dr. Watts operated and completely cured her disability, and Ratnamma sent the good news to her husband.

"And to-day," she added, "he has come to me loving and tender as of old and wishes to take me and my babe back to his home. Should not my face reflect the sunshine in my soul?"

Women of India—wives, mothers, widows—my heart bleeds for you!

Even the proverbs of India teach hatred and contempt for women. Here are one or two of the many:

"What is cruel? The heart of a viper. What is more cruel? The heart of a woman. What is the most cruel of all? The heart of a soulless, penniless widow."

"He is a fool who considers his wife as his friend."

"Educating a woman is like putting a knife into the hands of a monkey."

When a girl is born a wail goes up from the entire village who have been anxiously waiting for a boy, and curses and reproaches are heaped on the innocent infant head. Should you at such a time ask the parents if a child had been born to them, they would reply: "A child? No, it is only a girl!"

In former generations girl infants were murdered on the slightest pretext—because of a divine injunction; because of a superstitition that a girl baby murdered would return to earth a boy; because women, generally thought useless and expensive, were better out of the world; or because poverty would prevent the giving of a suitable marriage portion.

The baby is married, often to a man of middle age, and long before her half-grown body is prepared, she is brutally compelled to begin her marital duties, and, when yet in her own childhood, she becomes, at the peril of her fragile life, the mother of a necessarily fragile child.

If, through overwhelming misfortune, the girl's husband die, her sins in some former existence are supposed to be the cause of his death, and because of this she is an accursed thing. Even though but a babe and knowing nothing of the dead husband, she is, at an early age, stripped of all ornament, and put in the coarsest raiment, while her head is shaved close and kept that way. Despised, spat upon, cruelly overworked, starved, beaten, neglected in illness, forsaken even by those nearest of kin to her, the child passes her days in abject terror and despair, until death, usually not long delayed, blessedly releases her.

When a child is about to be born the expectant mother is thrust into the cowshed or into the hottest, closest room and the darkest and dirtiest in the house, to await her trial, and her life and the life of her unborn child are entrusted to the ignorant wife of the low-caste barber. With foul instruments she intrudes on nature's honest efforts, often when nature needs no assistance.

When need for assistance does arise, God pity the poor victim of the midwife's malpractice! The heartless brutality used is not a fit subject for print. It is enough to say that in such cases the babe often loses its life; the mother nearly always. It is customary in India to ask when one hears of the birth of a child: "Did the mother live?"

A slender little girl of ten was brought to the hospital by her husband, a tall, muscular man of forty. The child shrank piteously from the man, who held her firmly by the wrist, and she seemed overjoyed to leave him for our nurse, who led her into the examining room. When I learned that the merciless brute, transgressing even the lax Indian ideas of decency and justice, had compelled the consummation of marriage and had injured his child-wife so seriously that only a grave operation could restore her health, I felt like shouting aloud to all the women of the happy Western world to help me crush the evil system responsible for the soul-sickening condition of the little patient before me.

Scarcely able to control my indignation, I returned to the husband and bade him "listen to my words of wisdom."

"Do you wish a son?" I asked. That struck the right chord, and he replied: "Does not every man wish for that more than for aught else?"

"Then hear me!" and I proceeded to tell him simply and frankly why he was defeating his own object. When I had repeated and repeated my arguments, I had partly convinced his asinine brain—no, not "asinine," that were an insult to the worthy ass—that I was right, and he promised to show consideration for the helpless child in his power and to let her remain at our hospital for a time.

There is a hamlet about five minutes' walk from our compound where Brahmans only are allowed to live, and where there is a sacred bathing-well. In that settlement a wife of fourteen years was expecting immediate motherhood. Something was not right; there was alarming delay; and all the wisdom of the midwife and of the old men and women had been called upon to furnish help in the dilemma. As is usual in such cases, a ring of children, among whom were of necessity two boys bearing the names Rama (one of the names of Vishnu, God of Preservation) and Lakshmanna (the masculine form of Lakshmi, Vishnu's wife), encircled the well, and a brass bowl filled with the sacred water was passed from one child's hand to another's until it had gone the round three times. Meanwhile the suffering girl had been brought to the well and the boy Rama handed the water to her to drink. Even this charm failed; so at last they all admitted it would be wise to seek help from the foreigners.

I was asleep in my cot on the veranda when a man's voice aroused me.

"Please come quickly, Honorable Doctor Lady" —and the matter was explained to me.

In a moment I was ready and the messenger and I were on our way, when we met another man who told us there was no need of my services for the child was born and all was well. I went back to bed and heard nothing more of the case until five o'clock the following afternoon. Then a messenger came in haste and said that a lie had been told me the preceding night; that the child had not been born, but that they had wished to try, without my interference, another "trick," which was that a man should go quietly behind the patient's head without her knowledge and suddenly discharge a shotgun close to her ear. The "trick" had been carried out—the messenger continued—the dead child had been instantly born, and the young mother had screamed with pain for many minutes and then had gone into convulsions. When I arrived on the scene the patient was rapidly passing from one convulsion into another, and I saw instantly, and told the people, that the poor girl had been done to death. I stayed by her side until dawn, when her spirit took its flight from her tortured body.

> My God, can such things be!
> Hast Thou not said that whatsoe'er is done
> Unto Thy weakest and Thy humblest one
> Is even done to Thee?

XXIV

JUNGLE FOES

A WILD beast scare had stirred the whole district. In villages bordering on Medak three babies had been eaten by tigers. A leopard seized a sleeping boy and began to drag him to the woods. The boy's screams roused his father, who caught him by the legs and fought madly with the leopard for possession of the child. At last the screams of both father and son frightened the beast, and, letting go its hold, it fled. The boy's face was torn completely through from mouth to ear, and his father brought him to our dispensary at Surjanna, where Miss Posnett sewed up the wound, which healed nicely.

As Miss Tombleson and I strolled along the Ramyanpett road one day, a wolf came out and stood in front of us, looked us over calmly, and walked away again.

A few days later there was great excitement in the compound. One of our missionaries had seen a wolf sneak behind the cook-house, where, lying about in the hot night air, babies galore slept peacefully beside their mothers. The creature escaped before it could be shot and fortunately no harm was done. The wolf stories told by the people are most thrilling, and truly the beast has an ugly way of hunting. Finding an infant beside its mother, it creeps up in the dead of night and slowly and stealthily rolls the child away from its protector. Then the sharp fangs meet in the little throat, there is a quickly stifled cry, and the mother wakes to see her babe in the jaws of the wolf as he leaps away into the darkness. So the wolves, because of the secrecy of their attack, have come to be more dreaded than even the man-eating tiger.

Within a few days the wolf that had visited our compound came again, and fortunately one of the English gentlemen saw it in time and killed it with one shot. Then the people, wild with exultation, danced and sang and shouted for hours around the gaunt, gray body.

Two of our missionaries returning from Ramyanpett reported that a leopard had followed the *bandy* for some distance, leaving at last on the track of wild deer which had just gone on in front.

That was about the fifth time a leopard had been seen by our people on the Ramyanpett Road;

and one night a half-grown leopard sprang over our hospital wall and nearly drove the helpless nurses into nervous prostration by sleeping till the dawn in a vacant bed on the veranda.

It was after all this that I saw for the first time a wild leopard in his native haunts.

We were driving along the Ramyanpett Road, one of our pet terriers running behind the *tonga.* Suddenly the driver brought the bullocks to a halt, and, pointing to the bushes at the side of the road, whispered: "A leopard!" True enough! There in the grass, scarcely ten yards ahead of us, crouched the savage beauty, his head lowered and his eyes almost closed as he gazed fixedly at us.

I softly called the terrier to me, and, holding him fast in my arms, we waited, the driver's eyes and mine never leaving that mass of spotted velvet in front of us, until fully fifteen minutes had passed, when the leopard, doubtless tired of our monotonous standstill, deliberately rose to his feet, and, with an occasional bound from rock to rock, trotted slowly off into the deeper wood.

We frequently found cobras and other poisonous snakes in the bungalows. As I came out of my dressing room one day, a slight movement startled me, and there, not three feet away, a half-grown cobra was writhing. When I started at sight of him he raised his head, spread wide his hood, and darted his tongue at me with a warning hiss. I did not stop to cultivate his acquaintance further, but rushed out and sent the servants to kill him. When they arrived, however, he had escaped.

A cobra had to be chased out of the girls' schoolyard before they could begin afternoon session; and another cobra came, an uninvited guest, to Miss Tombleson's prayer-meeting for the coolie women. In the midst of the crude attempts at hymn singing and of the howls of the babies—a coolie woman always has a babe in arms—one of the women shrieked and stared at the ceiling. Following her gaze, the others looked up and there hung a cobra with a dead rat in his mouth. The weight of the rat seemed too much for the snake; he dropped his burden among the women, followed it, striking the floor with a thud, and then, himself thoroughly frightened, writhed swiftly down the steps and out of sight under the stones.

One market day as I stood near the dispensary veranda at Ramyanpett, listening to the singing of the Christians in the little chapel only a few yards distant, I saw an immense king cobra writhing along the ground close to the side of the chapel. Suddenly, to my horror, he raised his hooded head and looked in at an open window beside which a little schoolgirl stood, singing lustily. The snake's head was just back of the child's and not six inches from it. With a swift prayer that the child might not see the serpent and make a fatal move, I gave a low, shrill whistle. The snake turned his head in my direction, and as he did so I jumped toward him waving my arms. Instantly he dropped to the ground and sped into the long grass near by, while my brain swam with the joyful reaction.

XXV

NEW CAMPING GROUNDS

THE long Mahomedan and Hindu holidays and big feasts occur during the winter season, hence all the Indians are too busy merrymaking to attend to their sick relatives. When I told a Mahomedan gentleman that his granddaughter would die if they did not bring her to the hospital, he replied: "I believe you, Doctor Mem Sahib, but what can we do? We have no time to bring her now or to stay there with her. For yet many days the feast must be celebrated." This practical emptying of the hospital usually gave us an opportunity for medical touring, and one winter we planned to go to some town near the railway. Sending the other assistants ahead, and taking Abbishakamma with us, we boarded the train at Akanapett station.

One of our fellow passengers proved the first object of interest. Carefully hidden from sight behind her *bhourka,* it was only when we had passed the station and she had thrown back her veil that we saw how old and sad was her face.

With the usual idea of friendliness in India, Abbishakamma had soon drawn from the lady her story.

She was traveling to Hyderabad to take charge of the children of her daughter who had just died. The bereaved mother wept bitterly when she spoke of this tenderly loved daughter; how fair she was, how good and true, how intelligent! She had been "educated" and could read and write. "Oh, never before was so lovely a flower torn from its stem by the hand of Allah!"

As we left the car, the old lady, in extreme courtesy, slipped off her shoes and, standing upon the seat, bent almost double in her parting *salaam* to us.

Arrived at Wudrarum, we heard the loud wailing for the dead and learned that the *patel's* young wife had just died in childbirth. They were about to carry her to her funeral pyre, so, much interested in the funeral ceremonies, which we had never yet seen, we followed with the hundreds of villagers.

The litter on which the body was borne consisted of two long, parallel poles, to which were fastened transversely, with ropes of straw, seven pieces of wood. The shroud was wrapped around the body and bound strongly with straw ropes, the face left uncovered, and flowers scattered over all.

The relatives and friends and the villagers besides wailed loudly as the litter was carried along, the mother's wail rising shrilly above the rest:

> Oh! the apple of my eye; Oh, my darling; my blissful paradise.
> Oh! the apple of my eye, where hast thou hidden thyself?
> Oh! my flower, where hast thou hidden thyself?

and on and on in the piteous "Mother's Wail" which every Indian girl learns by heart in early childhood.

Three times the litter was placed on the ground and each time the mother wept and wailed and caressed the dead face of her beloved. At one of the halts all the jewels were removed from the body.

In an empty field on an oblong pile of fagots, constituting the funeral pyre, the corpse was placed. It was then covered with small splinters of wood, sprinkled with *panchagavia* (the five products of the cow) and soaked in oil. The husband, holding his eldest son—a boy of eight—by the hand, walked about the pyre three times, the boy allowing water to trickle from a cracked earthern *coonda* he held. At the end of the third trip around the body, the boy suddenly dashed the *coonda* to the ground, shattering it into hundreds of pieces, a symbol of the end of life. All this time the chief mourners and everybody else wept and wailed and struck the breast, or, in couples clasped in each other's arms, they swayed to and fro in the extremity of grief, or in the semblance of it in case of the hired mourners.

Now the boy took a lighted torch and set fire to the four corners of the fagot-pile. When the flames had caught, the family departed to go through with the long, tedious ceremonies following a death. The mother of the deceased must walk around the village for twelve or sixteen days, wailing always and calling out at every gate: "My child has gone from me!" So, with the bitter cry, "My child, she was my very own child!" the poor old creature departed on her weary round.

We watched the burning until the body was utterly destroyed, and when in the morning we came again the family were ready to gather the ashes and throw them into the Ganges, taking the long journey for the purpose, for they were wealthy people and could afford this "priceless blessing for the dead."

At the camp, a mother brought to us her baby boy, an only son, whose life might have been easily saved by a slight operation. When I explained this to her and begged her to bring the child to our Medak Hospital, she exclaimed: *"Mari yetla? Sanipotai, sanipotardoo. Adrushtam! Yami chayavallinoo?"* (And how? If he dies he dies! It is fate. What can I do?) Truly the overcoming of obstacles is no part of the Hindu nature.

The day following was a feast day, but that did not prevent the patients nor the officials of the village from coming to us, as usual. But ah, the splendor of these "great ones"! The blue and pink flowered satins; the rich velvets with silk embroidery; the elegant gold and silver bordered turbans! As frankly as a small boy displays his first trousers they showed us these fine garments.

"See!" they boasted, turning round and round for our inspection. "Are we not fine in our new clothes?"

Nothing could equal the careless grace of the tall pale *moonshi* as he tossed back his long hair in the evening breeze and posed for us. With much ceremony he informed us that they would immediately begin to collect the money for a dispensary, as they all were extremely anxious we should come to them once a week, and that they had planned to inscribe in large red letters to cover the entire outer wall of the building the words, "Doctor Mem Sahib!"

On this feast day presents poured in faster

than ever, if that were possible, for the *tahsildar,* the *peshgar,* the *moonshi,* and the *patel* had during our entire stay in their village vied with one another in providing us with foodstuffs of all sorts. When these gifts of food were presented, the long procession of servants, in their medley of bright-colored costumes, and bearing on their heads huge vessels of queer shape, brought vividly to mind the picture of England's Christmas in the olden days, "Bringing in the boar's head."

At Mirzapally, where we next went, black smallpox was working havoc in the village.

Poshamma, the goddess of smallpox, is considered by the Hindus an especially powerful devil goddess, and, as a rule, the Hindus refuse to give any form of treatment for the disease, for "Did not the goddess Poshamma send the smallpox? Shall we not offend her if we try to cure the victim of her displeasure?"

We were called to a hut where, when I had become accustomed to the smoky darkness, I saw on the floor two or three children in all stages of the dreadful disease. One, a child of three years, fairly putrid with the worst form of smallpox, lay with her head in the lap of an untainted girl of ten. In another hut a woman, stricken down by the black demon and fainting with weakness, suckled her healthy babe. Alas, poor India!

Mirzapally is on the railroad line to Hyderabad, so we snatched a holiday "in town."

We called on Mrs. Nundy, and then, in a hired *tonga,* drove to Secunderabad. Our driver's brutality to his skeleton horse so disgusted us that, after vainly begging him to stop whipping the poor beast with such unnecessary severity, I devised a preventive method. Every time the horse was struck I said nothing, but, much to the driver's amazement and in spite of his shrill protests, I reached over the seat and gave his bare arm a severe pinch—twisting, torturing! At last his dense brain grasped the "cause and effect" idea, and the horse was allowed to trot on unmolested, while the driver meekly nursed his bruised limb.

At the Secunderabad post office I asked the cost of registering a parcel "from Secunderabad to New York City." After a full hour's search for the information in question, the Hindu gentleman in charge of the registry department closed the books over which he had been poring, and remarked in a grave, emphatic tone: "Madam, you are mistaken in the name of the city. There is a New York State, but there is no such place as New York City!"

From Secunderabad we came back to Mirzapally and journeyed on to Sandampett. We were just settling ourselves to dinner the first evening when a tall form enveloped in a gray blanket fell at my feet, and in the patting and stammering which followed, I could recognize only that another grateful patient had found us out. Then he arose and we beheld the *patel* of the village, a handsome man of twenty-two, who, the year previous, had undergone a serious operation in our hospital. I recalled that when he came to us I had feared for his life; and it was a real joy to me to see, instead of the thin, hollow-eyed youth I had known, this fine, strapping fellow. He had forgotten not one of the kindnesses shown him in his illness.

"Did you not smooth my hair and call me your son? Did you not watch over me day and night with loving tenderness?"

And so, over and over, he enumerated every act of ours during the anxious time of his illness until our butler gently but firmly reminded him that it was eight o'clock and we had not yet dined. Then, reluctantly, he left us.

Our grateful *patel* had played "advance agent" to such good purpose that over three hundred patients came to us next day, the *patel* standing outside and urging the people to come quickly and in numbers.

"Do you fear the Mem Sahibs because of their white faces? There is no fear, I tell you; there is no fear! They work no evil; they work all good; they bring hope to the hopeless and health to the dying!"

The whirl of things kept us from realizing our weariness until the sun had gone down, when, with an involuntary sigh of relief, we saw the last patient depart, and started out for a little stroll on the banks of the beautiful lake back of the tent.

How can the Hindu be aught else than poet and dreamer with such scenes continuously before him?

On one side sparkled the broad, blue lake dotted with white water lilies and with wild duck by the hundred floating on its surface; on the other, huge, tumbled boulders gazed majestically down on dainty, blue grass-flowers and rich, purple convolvulus.

In the rice fields beyond row on row of women labored, chanting while they worked, their red garments in striking contrast with the green of the fields.

From this fair scene we strolled to the mango tope near our camping place, and until darkness fell watched the hordes of monkeys which romped unceasingly among the giant trees. These big monkeys, though amusing enough in their tree-homes, sometimes descend in great colonies upon a village, and then the destruction they wreak is frightful. In a few minutes a roof has its tiles completely off, or a large rice field has not a *dub's* worth of rice left in it.

Another rushing day was followed by another walk. As we turned back toward camp our path led along the high, narrow bank of the lake, which on one side sloped steeply to the water and on the other led sharply down twenty feet to a pile of rocks in the mango tope. As it happened, all the hundreds of monkeys had decided to occupy for the night a tree that hung over our path, and when we, of necessity, passed beneath them and so near that we might have touched them, their rage was unbounded. Amid the screaming and chattering of all the monkey colony, ten or twelve large males rushed down the limbs toward us as if they would tear us to pieces. We knew that the least sign of fear would probably be fatal, so past the blazing, green eyes, the fierce, white teeth, and the eager, clawlike fingers almost at our throats, we marched steadily with our heads high; but the thumping of our hearts nearly choked us, and when the danger

Watering the rice-fields

was past we sat down on the grassy bank white and weak and trembling.

At noon, next day, the jugglers and snake-charmers came—Hermanns without the stage-settings. They produced rabbits from nothingness; spouted fire from their mouths; raised mango trees before our eyes from seed to fruit; and charmed their glistening cobra-pets with the soft music of their pipes.

A babe of two was with them, and the bored look on the little face as he twined a cobra or python around his tiny neck or pulled it about as if it were an inanimate toy was comical enough.

It was the boy of twelve years, however, that held our gaze. His gypsy face, his tangled hair falling low over his shoulders, a dirty turban set sidewise on his saucy head, his ragged coat and *dhoti,* his nimble gestures, his bright, impudent smile, and the art in his voice as he played his part, bewitched us, and all too soon he picked up his queer, native drum and strolled away in the wake of his masters.

Two performing bullocks, great, beautiful beasts with the hump on the back much enlarged by vigorous massage from their youth, entertained us for a time. All decked with bright ribbons and little, tinkling bells, they chased playfully about the field after their master and pretended to gore him, or made deep *salaams* to us with knees bent and with head touching the ground.

As night came on we were about to move away, and already our tent was packed, when our evangelist said the people were begging us to stay and talk about our religion.

So down in the moonlight we sat, and as far as the evangelist's voice would reach were clustered men and women, all listening eagerly to his words, now and then nodding their heads intelligently or rubbing their hands with glistening eyes of assent to some special point.

One of the men came up to us and begged us to take his boy into our school. "Do you know," he said, "ten years ago white Padres came and talked to us of your Christ and we all ran away afraid of being cursed, and now if we dared we should all be Christians."

Then song followed story and story followed song, until we thought they would never be satisfied. At last, one by one, they straggled off, and by midnight all were gone.

At Kalvakoontla a warm reception greeted us from some grateful patients of old. As these "grateful patients" happened to be the chiefs of the village, they filled the tent, and when, after talking to them awhile, we begged to be excused, for hundreds of people were waiting outside for medicine, they laughed carelessly: "Oh, never mind those people, they can wait." Still we did manage by strenuous endeavor to treat practically all who came.

Kalvakoontla is a *jagir* village; that is, a village given by the Nizam to some one man for services rendered, and all the revenues of the village are thenceforward paid to this favored man, and all law is in his hands. In fact, the village is a tiny, independent state. Here the Dacoities and other bad men flock, for they are beyond the reach of law unless the owner of the village punishes them, and he has this power only if they commit the crime in his village. The *Jagadir* of Kalvakoontla was sick and had begged us to see him. A kindly old graybeard, he lay comfortably in bed on his veranda hid by vines from the street, and talked to us in a loud, cheerful voice.

"I have just a little fever; I wish you would send me some medicine," he said, as I felt his pulse.

"Have you had any medicines yet from the *hakims?*" I asked.

"Indeed I have not," he replied emphatically. "I'd rather die than drink black men's medicine," and he grinned round at the group of "black men" standing near, who took no offense but all grinned in response. "No, the only medicine I've had is cahster ile (castor oil)."

"All right, I will send you some medicine. By whom shall I send it?"

"Oh, by anybody; these people all belong to me."

The love of medicine runs in the Indian's veins. A naked baby of scarcely two years peeped shyly out from behind his mother's skirts and gravely offered me his hand.

"He has not been feeling well for a few days," said his mother. "He wants you to feel his pulse."

As we were leaving one of the villages, ten or more lepers, in all stages of the terrible disease, came to the tent and begged us to help them. We did what we could, but our hearts ached at the hopelessness of it all.

On the homeward journey, we passed through a remarkably clean and attractive village made up entirely of Brahmans and other very high-caste people. There was an eclipse of the moon that night and the caste people, after greeting us very courteously, asked us to tell them about the eclipse and its meaning:

"In your *shastras* (science or books of religion) what evil does such a thing as this predict? In ours thus and thus will befall."

We explained to them the scientific theory of the phenomenon, but we might as well have held our peace, for they only looked at us pityingly as if to say, "Is that all you know about it?"

XXVI

MAHORRUM

WHEN the great Mahomedan feast of Mahorrum comes to an end, the streets seem very dull after all the color and crowding and jollity.

The feast of Mahorrum is held in honor of the two sons of Mahomet, Hoseyn and Hassan, who were killed in battle. The feast also gives Mahomedans an opportunity to worship all dead heroes, and everywhere about the village effigies made of tall poles decked in gaudy cloth and tinsel represent these heroes and are worshiped as saints or *pirs*. On the last night of the feast the *pirs* are treated as real dead bodies, washed in the lake for purification, dressed in proper grave clothes, and buried with all ceremony.

Anybody who dies a death of violence is a "hero." An Arab who was killed last year in a drunken quarrel was one of the heroes this year and his *pir* was worshiped with the rest. One of the *pirs* was erected just outside our compound gate, and throughout the feast men and boys circled about the pole, waving palm branches and chanting loudly in time to odd Indian drums, "Hoseyn! Hassan! Hoseyn! Hassan!" over and over again.

The Mahomedans throw their whole souls into the celebration; dress their gayest, and laugh their jolliest. Boys and girls in gold and scarlet run through the village bubbling over with joy; for the streets are lined with booths where men sell the fruits and candy and toys which can be had only at Mahorrum time. Everywhere men and boys disguised as tigers or bears or monkeys frolic in the midst of real bears who dance clumsily at their masters' commands; while the drums keep up their monotonous "jinkity-jing! jinkity-jing!" Besides the drums, music of every variety known to the Hyderabad Indian fills the air. One instrument is somewhat like a bagpipe in appearance. One pipe is placed in the mouth of the player and one pipe in each of his nostrils, and the sound is like a flute accompanied by the humming of myriads of bees.

Of course, beggars abound, religious and otherwise, among the rest repulsive devil priests with long, matted hair and wild eyes whose bodies, splotched with green and red and yellow paint and powder, are saved from mother-nakedness by a scanty loin cloth. Leper beggars, too, are there, half eaten by their hideous sores.

On the fifth day of Mahorrum, in Hyderabad City, the procession of the Lungar takes place.

Two or three centuries ago, when the crown prince of Golconda was hunting in the forest, his elephant ran away with him and, as the rescuers started in pursuit, the distracted queen vowed that, if her son were saved, she would give to the shrine of Hoseynji Allum, the most sacred in the kingdom, a *lungar* (the tethering chain which encircles an elephant's foot) of pure gold.

The son was saved and on the fifth day of Mahorrum the Royal Family, their vassals and retainers, all in gala attire, carried the golden *lungar,* with much pomp and ceremony, to the shrine. On every anniversary since there has been held the *lungar* procession, all the troops of the Nizam, regular and irregular—about fifty thousand men—joining in the event.

The Irregular Troops are those of the feudatory princes, who, under a system somewhat like the feudal tenure of old England, give revenue and military service in payment for land held.

The Lungar is the greatest holiday of the year in Hyderabad, and the city gives itself up entirely to pleasure. People from the surrounding country swarm into the place by thousands, and the streets are a mass of many-colored life.

On Lungar day the Prime Minister is accustomed to invite to tiffin two or three hundred guests who witness the parade from the balcony of his palace. One year, through the courtesy of the chairman of our mission society, several of us received an invitation.

Our party was at the palace in good time, and, waiting for the procession, we laughed and chatted with each other, watched the gay crowd about us, and felt no impatience. Prince George and Prince Conrad of Bavaria were there, the British Resident and his family, and the officers and ladies of the Secunderabad garrison, besides many of the Civil Service people, for all the Hyderabad world turns out for the Lungar parade.

His Highness, the Nizam, was not in town; but in the private gallery next to us, which is always reserved for the Nizam and his family, sat the royal children. The boys gaily frisked about, but the girls, two mites of three and five, sitting quietly on chairs, while their *ayahs* slowly fanned them, were charming pictures in green and gold pajamas and slippers and long overdress of sparkling gauze reaching to the knee, with topees of green and gold to match the pajamas.

In the great courtyard below, where the procession enters, wheels and salutes the Nizam and the Prime Minister, the villagers were making merry with all sorts of buffoonery, the Mahorrum "Tiger" with yellow stripes, long tail, and the mask of tiger's face, being a special feature

Suddenly the courtyard cleared; the procession was drawing near.

The Rocketeers were in advance and as they reached the saluting point, they discharged their rockets.

Then came a number of elephants, fantastically painted in all sorts of color designs, with long saddle cloths of velvet and cloth of gold, and bearing on their backs carved howdahs of silver or gold containing the princes of the Dominions, dressed in richest materials of brilliant coloring, often in pure cloth of gold.

One two-year-old prince, sitting quite alone in his howdah, looked down gravely from his exalted position as if he fully understood the dignity of his rank, his many jewels and his scarlet velvet coat, embroidered in gold and with a wide gold border, flashing in the sunshine, which also lighted the gay trappings of the horses and riders of his dozens of attendants who rode close beside the elephant and watched anxiously their baby lord.

The Camel Sowars followed, the camels richly

caparisoned like the elephants, but their riders in costume somewhat quieter than that of the occupants of the howdahs.

The well-disciplined and smartly uniformed police force which followed rested us slightly before the Irregular Troops burst into view, Bedouins, Sikhs, Pathans, Nubians, Arabs and Afghans, horse and foot, jumping, dancing, howling, chanting, throwing weapons into the air or discharging their guns.

The performance of the Arabs reminded me of the Scotch Highlanders dancing the sword dance, but the Arab's dress is rougher, his gestures wilder, and his yells more ferocious.

Each body of Irregular Troops was commanded by its gorgeously costumed chief seated in a howdah on the back of an elephant as splendidly decked out as its rider. These chiefs were preceded by a native band of musicians whose ear-splitting "music" and Dervish dancing, with drawn sword waving in air, added to the excitement, until we grew almost dizzy with the never-ceasing whirl and light.

Then came the Regular British and Indian Troops, artillery, cavalry, infantry, all quiet and soldierly. The horsemen were splendidly mounted and their thin-limbed Arab horses pranced and danced in perfect time to the music of the band playing old, familiar tunes, "Swanee River," "See the Conquering Hero Comes," or "Johnny Comes Marching Home."

For three hours the procession trooped past, the leader of each division stopping in front of the palace, to salute the Royal Family and the Prime Minister.

Then it was all over, and we ate the cake and drank the tea of prosy modern life.

XXVII

AN APRIL HOLIDAY

BECAUSE the Indian climate was fast sapping her strength, Miss Richardson had to leave us for England and Miss Tombleson and I accompanied her as far as Bombay.

On our way we stopped at "Mukti," Kedgaon, to see the marvelous work of Pundita Ramabai among the child widows of India. A bullock *gharri* conveyed us quickly from the Kedgaon station to Mukti, where we were introduced to Pundita Ramabai, a hazel-eyed, curly-haired little woman, barefooted and dressed in a *sari* of coarse white muslin. After a pleasant chat with the Pundita and her charming daughter Manoramabai, we visited the various departments of the institution.

Our next stop was at Poona to see the mission work of the Sohrabjis, those wonderful sisters (children of Parsees converted to Christianity) who have been so successful in uplifting their countrywomen.

After dining with Miss Susie Sohrabji, whom

I had known in Philadelphia, we called on her mother and her sister Mary, both of whom possessed Miss Susie's charm of manner; and this family charm seemed communicated even to the big, amber-colored Persian cat who drew his claws gently across our hands in a caress or strutted up and down with his plumed tail proudly erect.

In Bombay we visited at the first opportunity the Parsee "Towers of Silence" on Malabar Hill.

With morbid interest we watched the vultures as they sat on the top of the white, rounded walls, waiting, waiting!

Then we turned cityward, gladly welcoming the sight of the blue waters of the harbor, and the exhilarating touch of the salt breeze—sure enemy to gloomy meditation.

Our next goal was Elephanta Caves. A steamboat leaves Bombay in the morning for the island on which the caves are situated and returns in the evening; but when we reached Apollo Bunder and saw the merry little *tom-tits* skimming here and there through the water we decided to engage one. It was a less easy task than we had imagined, not, however, for lack of boatmen. At the intimation that we wanted one of their boats, the men fairly swarmed about us. Through their excited jabber came one persistent, nasal whine,

"My name, Ibrahim 77; I your best man; you liking my boat, Mem Sahib!" until importunity won the day and, turning toward the owner of the voice, we requested him to prepare his boat for us. And we did not regret our choice, although "Ibrahim 77" made an earnest effort at, not "highway," but "waterway," robbery.

"You not giving me more money, I not taking you to the shore," he threatened.

We had been a few years in the Orient, and were old hands at the game.

"Very well," I laughed, "this is a jolly little boat; we can stand it as long as you can. We agreed to pay you so much and just so much will we pay."

Several more of his efforts were silenced by our laughing indifference; then he gave up and proved a good-tempered and obliging pilot.

As our *tom-tit* danced over the sun-flecked waves in the strong breeze, we filled our lungs with the long draughts of the salt sea air and sang snatches of song to pass the time; for the caves are seven miles out from Bombay.

At the island we were besieged by small boys who had for sale beetles of a glistening blue-green color; and tiny, golden wood lice. Miss Richardson bought two or three of the living jewels for her brother's museum.

We found the caves much like those at Ellora, only there were fewer at Elephanta.

These dingy rock temples are weird places with the monster faces of the stone gods peering out at you in the semi-darkness from every pillar and wall, like a band of misshapen giants stealing upon you unaware.

Refreshing ourselves with ginger ale from a small shop near the caves, we started on the long, wearisome walk in the hot sun, over the wide stretches of sandy beach, broken here and there by a tall and lonely palm tree, toward the landing of the regular steamboat to Bombay.

Now came the time of farewell. Mrs. Adkin and the children had come to Bombay previously to take the same steamship on which Miss Richardson was to sail; and Miss Tombleson and I, as we watched the gallant ship plow her swift way westward, felt desolate indeed, for, in the intimacy of lonely jungle life together, your friends grow very dear to you.

Before leaving Bombay, we called on several acquaintances and visited in the way of sight-seeing the Rajabai clock tower and the famous Victoria railway station. Then, purchasing at the large, well-equipped Crawford Market a basket of mangoes and pineapples for the Medak people, we began our homeward journey.

At one of the stations we saw two entirely different types of "holy beggar." One, a wild-haired, fierce-eyed *fakir,* sat cross-legged on the platform, with his torturing hooks and knives and bed of spikes beside him. The other was an old *Sanyasi* or Brahman, who had reached the "last life" on earth. A look of unutterable peace was on his face; in his hand he held an artistic little brass begging-bowl; while by his side stood his ever-present disciple.

XXVIII

SWADESHI

IN Hyderabad, we got but the lightest zephyr from the *Swadeshi* storm sweeping over India. "*Swadeshi*" means "our own country." The Indian people in various sections of the land are rising against their English conquerors, boycotting English goods and filling the magazines and newspapers with seditious matter.

The chief instigators of the trouble seem to be the Indian laborer, ignorant and emotional, whose handicraft has been superseded by machinery, and his living thereby taken from him; the men who feel that they have been wronged in not receiving an appointment after passing the Civil Service examinations; and those who, from selfish and corrupt motives, rouse in young, inflammable students a false "patriotism."

It is generally admitted, however, that bad industrial conditions are back of it all, and these conditions are daily growing worse and worse. While salaries and incomes are fixed by iron-clad custom, the price of supplies and the amount of taxes increase with the advance of civilization. Of laborers the world over, those of India receive the poorest wage in proportion to the cost of living.

Then, too, the tariff laws of the Government give no encouragement to home industries. It naturally follows that the frequent "cornering" of necessary food supplies, such as wheat or rice, means to thousands of families cruel hunger and want.

Much of the trouble comes also from an inherent lack of ability in the East Indian to overcome obstacles. But these obstacles are many and great. Chief among them are, perhaps, the laws of caste and of labor, fixed two thousand years ago and to-day rigidly adhered to by these worshipers of ancestors and of past customs. Every man must do the same work and in the same manner as his fathers have done. Should he attempt improvement—which he never does—he would be boycotted. Each separate occupation means a separate caste, and when an Indian loses caste he loses all. He is ruthlessly thrust out from his little world; his own family will not even speak to him; no one of his caste will eat or drink with him; and from everybody he meets with nothing but curses and contempt.

Another obstacle is the extreme illiteracy of the Indian. Of the entire nation, including the learned Brahman class, more than eighty per cent of the men and ninety-nine per cent of the women can neither read nor write.

Still another obstacle is found in the fact that two millions of "holy beggars" fasten their teeth like vampires into the throat of India.

Then, also, the continuous heat of his country and the general practice of endogamy, together with the semi-starvation of generations, have so impoverished the blood of the Indian peasant that often the mildest disease—a disease to which we of the West would give scarcely a second thought—conquers and kills him; he expects illness and is surprised when it does not come to him; he looks forward with apparent equanimity to his annual attack of dysentery and rheumatism with the rainy season and of bronchitis with the winter season; and when he does fall sick he expects death rather than life.

Besides all this, the Indian is improvidence personified.

Among Indian coolies, both husband and wife are wage-earners and work equally hard, giving all they have to the support of their families. Mr. Posnett, trying to raise the pecuniary level of the coolie, offered, instead of the universal twelve *dubs* (three cents) a day to the woman and sixteen *dubs* (four cents) to the man, to raise the woman's wage to sixteen *dubs*.

"What!" exclaimed the men, "shall our wives earn as much as we? No, indeed! The women would soon become hardened with pride. Pray leave us as we are!"

A man has often refused to accept as an inheritance a field of land unless he can sell it immediately, "because," he says, "I have already one field to till; it provides enough food for myself and my family when the rains are good. Another field means extra work and taxes, and, if there is food for to-day, why trouble about to-morrow?"

Therefore, any little mishap in the weather is tragic. Too little rain or too much means famine immediately and terrible suffering; and an empty purse meets the grievously burdensome, religion-compelled expense—often a year's income—of a wedding, a funeral, or a religious feast. Money must be borrowed at from twelve to one hundred per cent. What, then, can keep the Indian peasant from the clutches of the merciless money-lender, and the peasant's child from being sold as a bond servant or "slave of the soil" to pay his father's debt? What hope has he of better days to come when his daily food might be increased in quantity beyond a starving allowance, and in variety beyond rice or lentils or coarse grains; when his house might be built of something more substantial than mud; when his furniture might exceed a few cooking pots; and when an increased self-respect might expel a few millions of the vermin of every variety which infest with impunity his dark and suffocating hut? How can his view of life be other than sad-colored; and, in the midst of his difficulties, what can he do but sit inert uttering his hopeless, "What can I do? If I die, I die!" or kiss the white man's feet and beg for help?

Another mighty obstacle to the progress of the Indian is that he never seems to learn wisdom from precept, example or experience.

I had entered into conversation with one of our coolies who is more intelligent and progressive than most of our working-people. He spoke of the threatened Russian invasion of India.

"We should not object to the English Government," he added, "if it would free us from the greed of the money lender. Usury is the ruin of our country!" and he brought his fist down on his knee with emphasis.

A wild impulse seized me to experiment in this matter.

"Listen to me!" I said. "Let's try to get rid of

this sort of thing, at least among the people of our own compound. I will lend you money when you need it and you will pay me three per cent interest yearly, the interest payments to be made monthly, until, at your own convenience, you pay the principal. I will ask no security and no questions. Deal fairly with me, and I will deal fairly with you!"

The coolie grinned delightedly.

"Trust me, Honorable Doctor Lady!" he concluded.

The next morning he came to my door.

"Honorable Doctor Lady, I need ten rupees. According to your suggestion of last evening, will you lend me that amount?"

I gave him the money and explained carefully that he must, when he received his next month's salary, come to me and pay the interest on ten rupees in *cowries* (small shells, one hundred and sixty of which are worth one American cent).

The story of my unprecedented philanthropy spread rapidly throughout the compound and in a short time I had lent the fifty rupees which I had resolved to spend in learning whether the Indian peasant could be helped out of the grasp of the money lender.

A month passed and the interest fell due. The

interest on each rupee was less than one-twelfth of a cent, but no interest appeared. I called separately on each of the people to whom I had lent the money and asked them for the small interest due. Each one replied with profuse apologies that he could not pay the interest. Then to the coolie I had first helped I delivered a long lecture, telling him how his dishonest dealing with me had cost him more than he realized, and how he could have no more pity from me on account of the money lender's usury.

He listened respectfully and when I had finished replied, "Truly you have spoken, Honorable Doctor Lady. I have been dishonest. I have not paid you the interest as I promised, but I am your son, and I hope you will not refuse to lend me ten more rupees which I require to-day."

All that was months ago; yet never have I seen one *dub* of principal or interest from any of the people to whom I lent the money.

It was after this banking experiment of mine had failed that on a certain day one of our house servants came to me weeping piteously.

"Honorable Doctor Lady," he cried, "I can bear this no longer. Every time I pass the money lender's door, he abuses me with vile words because I cannot pay him five rupees I have borrowed from him. Pray, pray give me the five rupees that I may pay my debt to him and hold my head high among my people!"

I gave him the five rupees and he departed grinning widely. The very next day the same servant came again to me.

"Oh, Honorable Doctor Lady, the money-lender still abuses me. Pray give me five rupees that I may pay my debt to him and hold my head high among my people!"

"Why," I cried in astonishment, "only yesterday I gave you money to cover the debt which you said was all you owed him."

"Truly you have spoken," sobbed the graceless scamp, whose alcohol-laden breath came heavily to my nostrils, "but I spent that money for tobacco and other necessaries, and the money-lender still abuses me."

Reverting to the *Swadeshi* problem, you will agree with me, I think, that, considering the character and environment of the Indian, he seems ill prepared for a successful revolutionary movement against England.

When I was in Calcutta, I asked one of the most progressive and best educated Babus if he thought the Hindus could, were the Government turned over to them, rule successfully their own country.

"No," he replied emphatically, "not yet. Our

Hindu people are too weak physically, mentally, and morally. We are too diversified with our hundreds of different castes and different languages. The dissension and hatred among the various castes would be enough in itself to prevent a Hindu government from being successful. Then, there are the Mahomedans. Though there are five times as many Hindus as Mahomedans in India, the Mahomedans are physically strong —born soldiers—and in war they would conquer us. The English rule is just, far more just than Moslem rule could ever be; the Government gives to the Indian people many high judicial appointments in the civil service, and the lower class of executive appointments; some of the English people are very good and kind; but the English and the Indian are so different; they do not understand each other—and the English do not love us"—he smiled rather bitterly. "You will understand better what I mean if you will notice the concentrated contempt of the Anglo-Indian in his utterance of those two words, 'the natives.'"

XXIX

TO THE HILLS AWAY

AT hot weather holiday time, Miss Wigfield, Miss Tombleson and I set off for Darjiling.

We had long promised ourselves a visit to the "Marble Rocks" of Jubbelpore, so at Jubbelpore station we stopped off and began our ten-mile drive to the "Rocks."

A good driver, a speedy horse, and charming scenery made the way seem short. Swaying bamboo clumps formed long avenues, and groves, rich with fine mango trees, held colonies of monkeys, gray and brown, which chattered at us as we passed.

It was almost dusk when we arrived at the Nerbudda River and our guide hurried out the pleasure boat for the two-mile row between the cliffs of pure marble fifty to eighty feet above the narrow but "bottomless" river.

As we climbed into the big boat, a naked baby boy stumbled over the rocks behind us, sobbing wildly. On asking an explanation, we were told by the boatman that the child was his son and loved the boat-ride; that he wept because they were leaving him behind, "fearing he might annoy Your Honors." Of course, we told the man to bring the little chap aboard, and the fat urchin's beaming smile as he snuggled down in the bottom of the boat well repaid us.

Snow white, with streaks or splotches of red, blue, gray, black or yellow, the marble rocks glistened above us. On ledges of the cliff, ungainly baboons settled themselves for the night's sleep, their figures plainly outlined against the white of the marble. Countless swallows' nests were there, and bees' nests of enormous size. Our guide told us how a foolish soldier had fired his gun at a bees' nest, and how the bees had instantly attacked him and stung him to death, his companion escaping only by swimming the river and running through the woods at full speed, the bees several times almost conquering him.

At the end of the row, where the river narrows into a *cul-de-sac,* we climbed out and waited on the shore for the moon to appear. While we scrambled among the boulders and picked up specimens of the colored marbles lying all about, the boatmen climbed up the hill and, building a fire, sat down for a good smoke. Then after an hour of pitchy darkness, which we beguiled by singing, the great round face of the moon came peeping over the horizon. Higher and higher it rose and at last smiled full on the marble cliffs. Oh, that transparent brilliance! Shall I ever forget it, or the row back again with the glittering white walls of rock towering over us and throwing off sparks like diamonds where the marble was cut and broken?

In the morning we visited the Jubbelpore Thuggee Jail, one of the best known in India. In former years the majority of the prisoners were Thugs, but the jail at present holds criminals of all kinds, and excels in the manufacture of tents and carpets.

A courteous English official showed us over the place. Every time we came to a set of prisoners, they instantly placed their working implements on the ground and, squatting down, held their open palms up toward us until we had passed. We were told that this was to show the absence of any weapon of attack.

We watched with special interest the carpet weaving, and marveled as the skilful, swiftly moving brown fingers transformed the mass of colored thread into a rug of beautiful design.

Life in a jail like this must be rather pleasant to the Indian laborer that is not entirely abandoned to laziness. Nobody is taxed beyond his strength with work; all have good food; are kindly treated and their caste prejudices are respected; while the sick are cared for in a well-equipped hospital. The object of the superintendent is to keep the prisoners up to a certain standard of weight and health, to get the best work from them and the least possible illness. To an active Western man the lack of freedom would be the greatest drawback; but the average Indian is contented with a room six feet square in any location. The hard couches built up out of solid earth might also seem a cruelty to the Western mind, but the Indian at home sleeps on the mud floor of his hut. This seems to be a matter of preference, for, in our hospital, tape-strung cots, such as we ourselves slept on and considered somewhat Spartan, were provided for the patients, but, in the early morning, I often found that they had slipped from the cot to the floor; and, when I asked why, they would answer: "The cot is so soft, it makes my bones ache."

Here in the jail, as at home, the Indian has his blanket and a little straw if he wants it. The unhappiness of the Indian prisoner seems to come solely from the compulsion to steady if not hard labor; and in his absence from his family.

Leaving Jubbelpore, we came one evening at sunset to the Sakrigali Ghat and the Ganges

Tree ferns of India

River. That sunset was one of the most imposing I had ever seen, the whole western sky a glory of pink and purple, scarlet and gold.

Facing the lurid light the many "Faithful" on board the steamer—gray-bearded men, young lads and little boys—knelt side by side on the big deck and went through their elaborate evening supplication to Allah.

Odd-looking, square-sailed boats floated on the Ganges, and everywhere along the shore hundreds of Hindus bathed in the sacred river.

At Siliguri, where the real ascent of the mountain begins, the little Darjiling-Himalayan Railway train waited to take us and hundreds of other people up to the cloudland above, and soon the diminutive locomotive was looping, circling, and zigzagging in the most perplexing manner as it pulled us slowly up the mountain-track.

The forests were filled with beauties and wonders, lemon, orange, and fig trees, orchids, mighty bamboos, and the famous tree-ferns, which frequently reached as high as a two-story house, each frond being six feet or more in length. Then gradually we came to the plant-life of a cooler zone, the laurel, magnolia, geranium, the oak, and the chestnut, and, everywhere, the white, the silver, and the scarlet rhododendrons made the world delightful with their rose-like blossom and lemon fragrance.

One of the most amazing sights in these damp, moss-covered woodlands was the "strangler," a climbing tree which winds about some straight-growing tree, and slowly chokes it to death and crumbling ruin, the spiral, empty sheath of the deadly parasite telling the doom of its victim.

Our eyes searched vainly through the dense woods for any sign of the wild animals which are said to abound in these forests, when suddenly Miss Wigfield called out, "O girls, look! An elephant!" Quickly scrambling to Miss Wigfield's side, we eagerly gazed out but saw immediately the joke that had been played upon us and joined in Miss Wigfield's laugh at our expense. A tame elephant with children playing fearlessly about him lazily swayed from side to side in the dooryard of a mountain hut, while with a young tree which he had pulled up by the roots and now grasped firmly in his trunk, he scratched his thick hide with seeming deep content.

At Kurseong we thrilled with travel enthusiasm to know we were but nineteen miles from mysterious Thibet.

As we climbed higher and higher, the white purity of the cloud wreaths on the mountainside stood out strongly against the green of the forest, and, as we neared Darjiling, the mountain folk, with Mongolian features and sunny smile, gathered at every station to offer the tourists irresistible yellow raspberries in fresh green leaf baskets, irresistible, indeed, when offered by the children, who seemed to me especially attractive, not with the cherubic beauty of the Kashmiri child but with the engaging drollery of a Japanese doll, with almond eyes and tiny mouth pursed tight.

XXX

DARJILING

COOLIES by the score rushed up to us at the Darjiling station, and we gazed in wonder while our baggage was strapped to the backs of the apple-faced women, squat and sturdy; the pack supported by a strap passing across the forehead, so that the strain came mostly on the neck and shoulder muscles. Two steamer trunks, a Gladstone bag on top, and a large basket in one hand was an ordinary load. One woman carried a small upright piano, bending almost to the ground beneath her burden. The women are evidently schooled to this from earliest childhood, for even the toddling babes had each its little pack to carry.

The people of Darjiling are a rare mixture. It is the summer home of the Lieutenant-Governor of Bengal, and there is a large British population, among whom we made many pleasant acquaintances. But the natives of Darjiling far exceed the whites in number. All these mountaineers are of the Mongolian type: the lazy, jolly, honest Lepchas; the cruel and quarrelsome, but hard-working Bhuteas; the small-headed, cringing Thibetans; and the nobler people from Nepaul, of whom the Ghoorkas, probably the best soldiers in the world, form the highest class. All wear long, loose, cloak-like garments, belted in at the waist, and the women are loaded with heavy jewelry, the turquoise being predominant. All seem possessed of playful good humor and physical strength and courage, strikingly different from the gravity and timidity of the inhabitants of the plains. Even the children are fearless. On our mountain climbs we frequently saw the sprightly little ones playing about like kittens on the very edge of frightful precipices. I shall not easily forget the sick horror that filled me when, climbing up a path, I rounded a curve and saw, some yards away, a child about two years old, leaning forward and far over an unguarded cliff which fell away some three hundred feet to the rocks below. But the baby's mother gazed placidly at him from a short distance away, and, long before I could reach him, the child turned and toddled back to the maternal arms. Guardian angels, must, I think, be kept fully occupied on these mountaintops.

Our "boy," Paulmung, was a Lepcha, of expansive smile and explosive utterance. When

Paulmung made the simplest remark, we were invariably startled as if a child had sprung from hiding and shouted, "Boo!" But his innocent face, giving no indication of any attempt at frivolity, allayed our suspicions, and we commanded ourselves in time to make a dignified response.

There are several good English schools in Darjiling, and the climate agrees so well with the Western children that the schools have a large attendance of rosy-cheeked boys and girls, bright-eyed and energetic, who form a marked contrast to the pale, hollow-eyed, listless English children of the plains.

One of the attractions of Darjiling is the bazaar where the weekly market is held. There, among the laughing, tumultuous throng, one may see every product, human and otherwise, of these mountains. Especially interesting to us was the "butterflyman's" box of Nature's jewels, for there are about five thousand varieties of butterflies and moths in the Darjiling District, many of gorgeous beauty. Perhaps the mountain air made us almost as much interested in the luscious *papois,* a kind of melon, which we would carry home by armfuls, always to find on eating them that we had not brought enough.

Snowy mountain peaks extended all around

us, but they were often obscured by the rain clouds which are thick at that time of year, and it was many days after our arrival before we saw Mt. Kinchinjunga, which, when not dimmed by clouds, is the glory of Darjiling scenery.

The hope of seeing Kinchinjunga by the sunrise light lured us to a night excursion up Mt. Senchal, a fine viewpoint. At three o'clock in the morning we started off for the long, dark walk.

On the top of Senchal we crouched down behind a low wall to avoid the bitterly cold wind, and waited for the sunrise. As the light grew in the east, we peered forth from our protecting wall to see if the day were clear. Not a cloud in the sky, and the light grew and grew, till the far-reaching snow line burst upon our vision! Mt. Everest was there, but the one hundred miles of distance reduced his imperial height until we could not surely distinguish him from among the many other thumb-tips of snow which he resembled. But Kinchinjunga! Superbly proud, supremely fair, she rose above them all! Silent, awestruck, we watched while great bands of color heralded the sun. One by one they covered the mountains until the majestic, cleft peak of Kinchinjunga, and even her glaciers and icy crags, were plainly visible. Rose pink, clear gold, rich purple, they glowed; then, softly, softly, lavender, silver gray, delicate amber, and the faint blush of the apple blossom. Now over the mountains came the sun exulting in his handiwork and smiling proudly down on those loved children of his, who, of all on earth, lie nearest to his heart, until they flashed back at him such radiant glances that we turned away with dazzled eyes.

In making the homeward trip, we took a shorter but rougher path down the mountainside through woods where were orchids by the hundreds hanging among the limbs, and where the continuous dampness had so clothed the trunk and branches of every tree with moss that it seemed a great forest of nothing but moss and orchids.

As we came out into the highway, we saw fluttering in the wind, from the branches of the trees, hundreds of Buddhist prayer papers, short, thin strips of paper in block type which are hung on trees so that the wind may blow the sentiment to heaven. All the prayers have one wording, *"Om, Mani Padme, Om!"* which, translated, is, "Hail to the Holy One whose jewel is the Lotus! Hail!"—the "Holy One" meaning Buddha.

Reasoning that the prayers would be wafted

upward just as well if a few of the papers were in our private possession, we climbed the bank and brought away a handful of the curious strips.

We sought out the Bhutea *Bhusti* (village), where the temples of the Thibetan lamas are located. The first sight that greeted us was the prayer-pole of the Buddhist. These poles were numerous throughout the settlement with their fluttering paper rags which are supposed to keep away the evil spirits. The clownish lamas, not in the least resembling *Kim's* gentle, dignified, old saint, show you their treasures with childish delight: the dirty idol, dressed in cheap tinsel, the great chair, with torn, soiled covering, on which sits the Grand Lama, and the trumpet made of a dead lama's thigh bone hollowed out and one end pasted over with tissue paper. We gazed with more interest at the collection of ancient Sanscrit writings wrapped carefully in cloths, and at the ponderous "Wheel of Life."

In the vestibule were two or three large prayer wheels, cylinders mounted on long sticks and filled with prayer papers. The lamas turn these wheels rapidly, a bell sounding at each revolution, and repeat monotonously, but with a wide grin, *"Om, Mani Padme, Om!"* We gave the first lama a fee for saying his prayers for us, but when all the other lamas rushed up and begged us to pay them for saying their prayers, we refused.

Climbing up the hill again to Darjiling proper, we stopped to watch the people weaving, with their simple, hand-made tools, the strong Thibetan cloths which are highly prized throughout India.

Desiring to see at close range a tea garden, we visited "Happy Valley," one of the many tea gardens of the district. Captain Keble, the genial proprietor, took us through the plantation, showing us the garden and the up-to-date factory, and making the various processes clear to us.

Before we finally left Darjiling, we had several more glimpses of Kinchinjunga from various points, one with the brilliant moonlight full on the snows—a vision ineffably sublime and so far above our horizon that it seemed more of heaven than of earth.

On our journey down to the plains we all, with one accord, voiced Mr. Ruskin's sentiment:

"The mountains seem to have been built for the human race, as at once their schools and cathedrals; full of treasures of illuminated manuscript for the scholar, kindly in simple lessons for the worker, quiet in pale cloisters for the thinker, glorious in holiness for the worshiper."

XXXI

HOSPITAL LIGHTS AND SHADES

WE were at dinner in the Medak bungalow when there stepped into the room a tall figure. His right thumb, severed near the wrist save for half an inch of skin, hung loosely from his hand, the blood spouting fiercely. He was so smeared with blood that until he spoke I did not recognize him as our own Arab *peon,* Ibrahim, usually the most immaculate and dandified of fellows. In a drunken quarrel, his father had struck at his heart with a sword. With upraised arm, Ibrahim had warded the blow, and, although he had saved his life, he had received several severe gashes. As I rushed him to the hospital for treatment, the father ran up and begged me to make his child well!

Ibrahim's thumb soon became as good as new except for a slight stiffness, though I fear he still disobeys the Prophet's teachings in regard to alcoholic beverages.

Every day the unyielding rigidity of the caste

system was thrust upon us. Narsamma, an old beggar woman of the goldsmith caste, one of the highest, fell and broke her leg, terribly lacerating the flesh. She was brought to us with the wound in the shocking condition usually found in the East—plastered over with cowdung poultices and riddled with maggots. The poor creature's system had become so saturated with the poison that she was too ill to hold up her head. Her caste people who had brought her to us promised to provide her with food, as we knew she would take nothing from our Christian hands. For a few days all went well, then her erstwhile caste friends said: "We have done enough for her; she is nothing to us," and they refused to bring more food. When I told her she would die unless she would accept food from us, she replied simply: "I cannot break my caste." So we sent messengers to Medak begging the village goldsmith to give us food for the sick old woman. In this way we succeeded in getting enough for her and Narsamma became well and fairly strong.

Two months later she came back to us, plump and smiling, to bring us a thank-offering of rice and flowers.

A lovely young girl led her mother into our hospital courtyard. It was pitiful to see the elder woman's panic and terror and to hear her shrieks: "Oh, the dreadful white faces! The dreadful white faces! I am afraid!" But the daughter smilingly soothed her, saying: "Don't be afraid, little Mother! They won't hurt you; they will make you well." At last we learned the trouble. The mother was suffering from a horrid cancer of the breast. It had been neglected so long that it required very careful treatment, and after an operation I kept the patient in the hospital for several weeks. During that time she learned to love and trust us. About four years later, this same woman staggered into the dispensary, looking so wan and sad that my heart sank, for I felt sure the dreadful disease had returned.

"No," she said, showing me the straight, clean scar where the cancer had been, "I have not come for your medicine but for your love," and she threw herself into my arms and wailed out her sorrow.

Her daughter, while performing some simple household task, had suddenly dropped dead. We remembered well the gentle, beautiful girl, and we grieved with the heartbroken mother. This high-caste Hindu woman had walked alone twenty-two miles through the jungle, fording deep streams and braving the hot sun and the

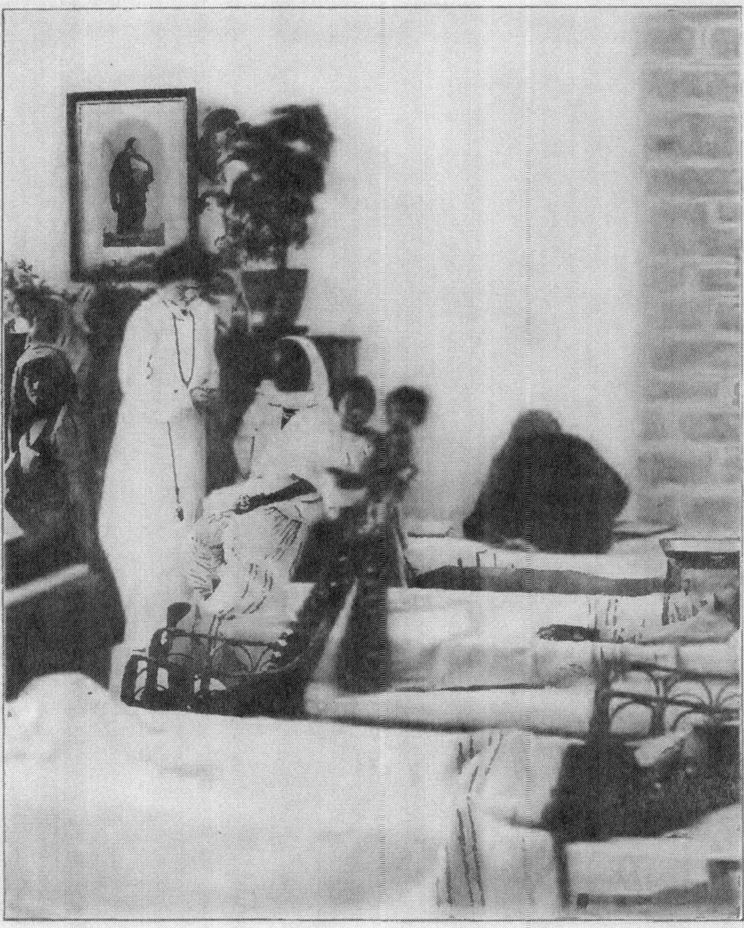

Medak Zevana Hospital, prayer corner, surgical ward.
Dr. Munson with patients.

wild beasts, simply that she might hear us tell her that we loved her and were sorry for her.

I had heard much in the West of the oriental lepers who kept a distance between themselves and the rest of the world by their cry, "Unclean! Unclean!" but in India, though a man be positively falling to pieces with leprosy and yet have money enough, many a girl is glad to marry him. Almost every day I treated lepers at our hospital, and I never noticed the slightest shrinking on the part of their friends who had come with them.

A leper woman, the wife of the richest man in Ramyanpett, came to our hospital; her attendance was of the best, her palanquin of the most luxurious, and her silks and jewels of the choicest, all this in sad contrast to her face eaten away with the dreadful disease, the blurred eyes, the ulcerating hands and feet, the awful stench of leprosy uncleansed. Even as these thoughts came to me, she stepped forward; and, *salaaming,* embraced me heartily. I succeeded in my effort not to shrink from her, but, like *Lady Macbeth,* I felt that not even the "perfumes of Araby" could ever make me quite clean again.

As I heard her story of distress and discouragement, my eyes filled with tears and my throat ached with a longing to weep with her; nevertheless, I could but marvel at her companions, as they sat beside her, one with her arms about the leprous woman's neck and the other resting against her knee, fanning her vigorously, neither seeming to mind in the least the close contact with the unfortunate creature.

The prevalence of hydrophobia among the pariah dogs gives rise to many cases of this terrible disease in the village people; but, with their usual fatalism and lack of imagination in regard to the future, the wound caused by the bite of a dog suffering from rabies is carelessly treated, if it be not altogether neglected.

One of our coolies, a lad of thirteen, when bitten by a mad dog, cauterized the wound with a burning torch and told nobody about it. A month later, his mother brought him to us in the last stages of hydrophobia. She was a widow and he her only son. In the West that would mean much, but in India it is all; the son provides for his parents in their old age, and is the one being who can pray their souls into paradise after death. I told the mother as gently as I could that her boy would live but a few hours longer. She gazed at me a moment before she comprehended. Then, with a look of the wildest anguish and before any of us could prevent her, she rushed to the side of the struggling, panting victim of rabies, and placed her arm over his frothing mouth. Again and again he savagely bit the limb. The poor mother shrieked with hysterical laughter at the sight of the dripping blood; and so, laughing and sobbing, beating her breast and tearing handfuls of hair from her head, she was led away by the village friends who had come with her. I had begged them to let me treat her wounds, but they refused, saying: "Why should she live? Will there be aught in life for her when her only son is dead?" While my professional spirit urged me to save her life, my woman's heart told me they had spoken well. But hospital scenes are not all so darkly shaded. One day a palanquin came swinging into the compound on the shoulders of four bearers, chanting as they walked.

A young princess from Hyderabad had come for medical treatment. Her costume of silks and velvets and jewels brought out strongly her Eastern beauty; and her tall, handsome husband, riding beside her on a spirited Arabian horse, added, in his splendid costume, just the right finishing touch to the picture. The moment I saw the *begum* with her shy smile I loved her; and I shall not soon lose the memory of her charming manners and affectionate gratitude. When she laid her head on my shoulder in a farewell embrace, she said: "In Hyderabad they told me that the foreigners would kill me. I answered: 'I have seen their smiling faces; they would kill no one.' Still I was afraid until I felt your loving arms about me. Now, behold! I am well and strong. Chee! (snapping her fingers in the air) I am not dead. I am full of life and happy, happy!"

The *begum* before she left us paid well for her treatment, and a few days later an immense basket of fine Hyderabad fruits came for the Mem Sahibs. Not all the thank-offerings of the Indian people were so acceptable. Sometimes they would put a strong-smelling, oily brown perfume on a bit of cotton and stuff it in our ears or smear it over our fresh shirtwaists till we were sights to behold. Sometimes they would take a rose or other flower and, breaking off the stem to within an inch of the petals, fasten it behind our ears or inside our neckbands.

Two hundred and sixty-three miles by train and jungle cart, the daughter of a rich merchant had come to Medak to receive our treatment; for, two years ago, when she was in great peril, God had given her life at our hands. This time the peril was more to her unborn child than to her.

"Why doesn't the doctor do this and this?"

whispered the patient's friends, naming the incantations and barbarous procedures common in such cases, or "The doctor will kill her, let us take her away," and the like, but through it all came the gray-haired mother's trembling, half-doubting tones, "No, no; she saved my child before; let us trust her now"—and then came the blissful moment when the nurse placed a fine baby boy very much alive in the arms of the rapturous grandmother.

With a great clanking of jewels and rustle of fine fabrics, Kulsimbhi's family entered the hospital, Kulsimbhi carried gently in their midst. Her left ankle, swollen to four times its natural size, was fairly riddled with maggots, and she was extremely emaciated and dangerously weak.

While we discussed her case, the *pahn* boxes were opened and all set to chewing on the *pahn* (a betel leaf filled with betel nut, cardamom, pepper leaf, and lime of the mussel shell, all folded into a tiny packet fastened with cloves).

I feared Kulsimbhi might lose her foot altogether, but careful examination showed there was hope of saving it. After the operation, she felt so much better that for many minutes she laughed and wept for joy, declaring that our name should "spread over the earth in its greatness."

The foot healed at last and, though Kulsimbhi was still very weak, I felt that she could be safely discharged from the hospital.

Months later, she came again to see us, and I should never have guessed that the brisk, young, bejeweled beauty, who tripped lightly into the courtyard, her eyebrows and eyelashes black with antimony, her forehead and cheeks yellow with saffron specked with gold leaf, and her nails red with henna, was the sad-eyed, tired little Kulsimbhi of former days. She was plump and good to look upon and her foot was absolutely well, the only sign of the old disease being the white scar line left by my knife.

My heart was especially glad when I could discharge, "cured," one of my worst hospital cases, a Mahomedan boy who, falling from a tree, had suffered severe concussion of the brain. He had been unconscious for three days when he was brought to me, and such a bruised, swollen head! Many a sleepless night hour I spent in my anxiety over him; but slowly improvement set in; a smile came to his mother's eyes, red and sunken with constant weeping; and three weeks after he came to us he was as dear and bright a twelve-year-old as you could have found in Medak. I called him *"Chota Sepoy"* (little soldier) because whenever I en-

The country cart stopping at Medak Hospital

Medak touring outfit

tered the room he would rise with a smile and a most military salute, "Salaam, Mem Sahib!"

As his family left us for their village, fifteen or twenty miles away, his mother drew her hands softly over my cheeks, in a pretty, Indian form of caress.

"When I started to bring my boy to you," she said, "all the village people cried: 'He is dying; if you take him to the foreigners they will kill him more quickly, that is all. Their medicine is not for us!' but I brought him in faith, and now, behold! I will show the village people what you have done and will say: 'See my boy! Did the foreigners kill him? Did they? No, they are more kind, more tender than a mother!"

But it is useless to make a reputation in India. A few weeks after this some people who had heard of the boy's cure brought us an old lady of eighty who had broken her hip two years ago and had not walked since, and a boy born deaf and dumb, for "Thou art like unto Allah," they said with bowed heads and clasped hands. "Even the dead rise at thy touch."

Baby Prema Divanna had been a pet throughout the compound ever since her history began.

Before her birth, her mother, a Brahman woman of middle age, came to the hospital accompanied by a white-haired Brahman widow, her adoptive mother, who told us that ever since her adoption the younger woman had been in disgrace of one kind or another, and she now wished to hide the illegitimacy of her child, whose father was a temple priest. Notwithstanding all this, the old woman waited as patiently and tenderly on the selfish, whining creature as an own mother might have done.

One evening as the orthodox Brahman widow, shivering in the chilly air, with her one thin white garment drawn closely about her, crouched in the corner of the hospital veranda that had been set apart for her, we ventured sympathy: "We are very sorry all this trouble has come to you and made you sad."

"To me," she replied with a patient gesture, "is no happiness and no sadness. I merely exist."

She told us then that the ten children who had been born to her had died and that she and her husband had gone on a pilgrimage to the shrines of India; that after her husband's death she had adopted the girl, who, later, had brought her so much trouble.

"Do you believe that after your death you will see your husband and children?" we asked. "No," she replied decidedly, "not my children certainly. They were merely loaned to me;

where they are now I do not know. My husband? Perhaps I shall see him, but from afar, for as he is a man he dwells near the gods."

A few nights after this the old lady, becoming worried about her daughter's condition, took her little oil-lamp and an offering of rice into the garden, and, prostrating herself, called loudly on "Jesus Christ, the God of the Christians." It was by no means a conversion to Christianity, but among her millions of gods she was adding, for policy's sake, the God of the people who were ministering to her daughter in her illness. The daughter herself was calling on her own god, "Oh Siva, Siva, Siva!" when one of our nurses said, "Don't call on the Hindu gods! Tell your troubles to Jesus Christ!"

"Who?" inquired the woman. The nurse repeated the name and gave a short explanation of what the name meant. Without comment the heathen woman continued her wail, "Jesus Christ, Jesus Christ!"

After the child was born the nurse told us that the mother had resolved to kill it at the first opportunity. However, we watched the baby carefully, and when the time came for the patient to leave the hospital I said to her: "Will you sell your baby to me for two rupees?"

"Sell it!" she replied. "I will pay you two

rupees if you will take it and save me the trouble of casting it into the river." So the baby became ours and we named her Prema Divanna (Love's Blessing).

Inherently superstitious, the Indian people find strange ways of deceiving the devil-gods whom they fear with pitiable terror. A Brahman woman brought to our hospital her ten-year-old daughter who was suffering from so slight an ailment that I was surprised when the mother fell at my feet in great agitation and begged me to save the life of her child.

"Oh, save her! Save her! Save her!" she cried hysterically. When I at last made her understand that her daughter's life was not in danger, I asked her why she was so troubled about such a light matter.

"Do you know my child's name?" she inquired tragically. "It is Adivi!"

"Adivi" means "jungle," or, in American parlance, "backwoods," and I marveled at the answer, for the Brahmans usually name their children for some goddess, or give them some such name as "Moonbeam," or "Lotus Lily," or "Jewel."

"Adivi!" I repeated. "Why have you given her such a name as that?" Then she told me her story:

"Sons and daughters were born to me and I gave them beautiful names and loved them. The Devil grew envious and took them from me. Then this daughter came and I said to myself, 'I will name her "Mistress Dung-heap," and will drag her through the filth of the stable, for then surely the Devil will never know I love her.' But I could not bring myself to this. I compromised; I named her 'Jungle' or 'Useless Earth,' and now, even now, see, I tremble for fear she also will leave me!"

In a few days, however, the girl was quite well, and the mother, in a grateful farewell to me, cried out the Indian form of blessing, "May you have seven sons and may your stomach always be cool!" (May you never have fever!)

The first attitude of the Indian people toward us is usually an attitude of suspicion and dislike. We are foreigners; we are white; we are different. Some of the people even go to the trouble to preach distrust of us in the open bazaar. We had an enemy of this sort in a young man whose father was a *hakim*. The influence of this youth, who could not say enough against us and against our hospital, kept hundreds of patients from coming to us. His sister, a girl of fourteen, became ill with typhoid fever; the *hakim* father happened to be out of town, and the frightened mother brought the child to us. She had been in our hospital one night when the father returned. He was very angry and demanded his daughter. I told him plainly that only Western treatment could save his daughter's life, and begged him to leave her with us. He replied:

"You will murder her; I shall have her well and strong within a few days."

He took the child from us, and in just three days she died.

Months passed and I saw nothing more of the *hakim,* but his active enmity and his son's continued. Then, again, one evening the *hakim's* wife came to me, weeping bitterly.

She said her grandson was dying; that they had done everything to no purpose, and begged me to help him. The sick child was the newborn and only son of my worst enemy. As the little creature had been born prematurely, and weighed only two pounds, it, of course, required very special warmth and care, but I found it lying on the mud floor of the hut without a stitch of covering on its body, and with all the winds of a January night—and January nights in India are cold—blowing over it. The babe was chilled to unconsciousness. I seized it at once and, holding it close to my breast, ran for the hospital. For hours I thought the wee boy would never again open his eyes, but at last the treatment took effect and he stirred cozily in his warm blankets. Then how we fought for that little life!

We made him a pretty "Baby Bunting" suit, a coat reaching to the feet and high boots reaching to the hips, both of baby blue flannel interlined with an inch thickness of cotton wool, lined and piped with baby blue silk, and tied with baby blue ribbons. With the aid of these doll clothes and of three warm blankets, we kept the baby's temperature up to the proper mark; and, knowing that if a moment's carelessness occurred the little flicker of life might die out, we carefully and personally supervised everything done for him.

Through it all we had to contend with the tearful resistance of the baby's family, who did not quite dare to take the child from us, but who daily prostrated themselves at our feet and begged us to conform to their customs in the treatment of the babe. My reply was always the same: "Your customs were killing him. Let us try our customs!"

At the end of three months, when the hot weather made it safe to do so, I gave him back, plump and bonny, to his parents. When I left

Medak he was a sturdy little son of whom any Indian mother might be proud; and the saving of his life gave his parents full faith in us.

As proof of this faith, the young father, shortly after I had resigned the baby to his own people, brought me his wife who was seriously ill. As he laid her on the bed before me, he said in trembling tones: "She is your daughter. I leave her with you in faith and hope."

When, well and happy, she left the hospital, the young man fell on his knees and kissed my feet, sobbing out his gratitude.

We have no warmer friend in India this day than our once arch-enemy.

It seemed to me that Ramamma would never recover her sight. Ramamma was a Hindu lady of nobility who had been blind for a year and had been treated for two months in our hospital. Then came a day when dimly but surely she could see. Slowly her sight returned, and we rejoiced with her happy family and her happy self.

Her husband and son, a precocious boy of twelve years with an almost English face, proudly brought us an Indian pony as a present. The man *salaamed* courteously as he presented the pony; but the boy, more profuse in his gratitude, finished a long presentation speech by suddenly prostrating himself at my feet. I was not prepared for this action, and, as I stood, one of my feet was in advance of the other. The youthful courtier looked up helplessly: "Why, Honorable Lady Doctor, how can I kiss your feet when they are not together? Put them together, please."

As I obligingly brought my feet into close apposition, he grasped them and holding them tightly, he gently bumped his forehead on them several times.

The phrase in Scripture, "because of his importunity," I readily understood after a brief acquaintance with a certain impudent, lovable knave, the ten-year-old son of Rassalbhi, a Mahomedan woman, who for many years had patronized our Temple of Healing.

In the midst of afternoon work at my desk comes a voice over the lower half of my door:

"Salaam, Doctor Mem Sahib! Will your Honor from the greatness of your heart grant to me, Hassan, the son of Rassalbhi, one small request? My mother has for many long days felt weakness upon her and she wished me to fetch her the strength-giving medicine which I was to call for last month."

"But," I expostulate, knowing that his mother's condition is far from serious, "why have you come in the afternoon? I have often told you that the dispensary is closed in the afternoon; you know I am busy with other work at that time; and when you live so near you should come in the morning."

The solemn, oriental eyes take on a reproachful expression.

"I make to you a thousand salaams, Doctor Mem Sahib! I kiss your feet; I am your slave; will your Honor give me the medicine?'

For five minutes I reason, command, threaten, not dreaming to escape the dispensary, but hoping to make him admit his error. His reply is unvarying and beyond argument: "A thousand salaams! Will you give me the medicine?" My time is precious and, as I have often done before under like circumstances, I surrender ignominiously. When I hand the boy the filled bottle, he promptly asks me if I will give him a pair of shoes. In spite of his mother's urgent need of medicine he seems to have no intention of hurrying home.

"These are excellent shoes," he declares, spying my bedroom slippers. "I should like these."

"But they are much too large for you, child."

"Oh no, they are very elegant!" and he clumps around in them with manifest enjoyment.

I do not yield to him so readily in the matter

of shoes as of medicine, but let him clump while I go on with my work; for I soon learned by sad experience the value of the Western shoe and clung desperately to the remnants of mine. Although your Eastern shoes have a number of fine points, they stick up so aggressively through the heel that, in the absence of any trustworthy cobbler, it requires at least a folded postal card to keep them properly modified. The soles are slightly less than an inch thick—saving in leather is no object—and some day when, your full trust reposing in those shoes, you have walked half a mile along a damp road, you feel a sudden and unusual sense of lightness and ease. Looking down you find that the sole has been left behind in the last mud puddle, and you sigh over the inadequacy of India's glue. One ought not to complain, I suppose, when the shoemaker will sit down on your back veranda—the shoemaker is the outcaste of India and is not allowed to sit on the front veranda where the *dhirzi* or tailor, a high-caste man, has his sewing machine—and make you any number of shoes at only sixty cents a pair with all that extra leather of the sole thrown in.

Queer and original ideas the patients sometimes gain from the Bible stories. We asked an intelligent high-caste Hindu woman, who had spent a few days in our hospital, to tell us the story of the Prodigal Son. This was her version:

"A man had two sons, and the younger son asked his father to give him his portion of the inheritance. This the father did. Then the son went to a far country and rapidly squandered his money in gambling, drinking, and a bad life. Finally, with the few rupees he had left, he bought china and set up a china shop in the bazaar. But he was very lazy and fell asleep. While he was asleep he stretched out his foot and lo! the china fell to the ground and broke into little pieces. Then what should he do? He was obliged to ask employment as a swineherd. But he had not enough to eat, so he stole for himself the food of the swine. The master, having noticed that the swine grew thinner and thinner, spied on the bad son, and found him eating their food. Whereupon he gave his unfaithful servant a great blow and a painful, which brought him to his senses, and he said to himself, 'I will arise and go to my father,'" the narrator completing the tale as it is written in the Scriptures.

A Brahman woman who heard the story remarked: "It is a good tale and well told. The Hindu religion is ours and so we pray to our own gods, but your religion is better, for, see, will a Hindu father forgive a son that has dishonored him? No! When anybody is in trouble, do our people give him help? No, indeed! They speak fair words from the *shastras* and tell him to go. Those who have much keep it all to themselves like a lamp hid in an earthen pot, but the Christians put their light on high places and it shines on everybody with love and kindness and good gifts."

Every one of my readers has at some time, I suppose, laughed over English as spoken by the East Indian.

These are letters that have come to us from our patients:

From Hyderabad.

To THE DOCTOR MEM SAHIB,

MY DEAR RESPECTED MADAM,

HONORED SIR,

I most humbly and respectfully beg to state a month past that I received a letter from my relation containing with following subject—that your husband has a pimple in his chest and he is dangerously ill, come as soon as you can possible. So at once I started from Medak to City without your embracings and kind permission. Please excuse me, I will come again near you, after the operation of my husband's pimple, because I had got the most satisfaction that your good remedy about the pain of my liver. You must send the reply to the following address:

Your most humbly and faithfully,

(Signed) O. K. —

Ramyanpett.

Great and Respected Queen,
My dear Sir:

Send advise written plain and quick by my *chaprassi*. I show my not having much sense one day because as I was going to see Tanks through the jungle, I felt very sick and tight. My servant said to me, Sir, lie down and I will give you berries from a tree, then all tightness will go. My respected Doctor Lady, my servant's words came true. I did eat and my whole Enatomy had never tightened since. Send your valuable drugs to make me tight again. I am lying down with no more strong on one side than the other side. Feet and legs to will not obey too quickly. No much life in my body.

Yours most humble and faithfully,
(Signed) ——————

A healthy looking, young Mahomedan called at the dispensary one day and made the following startling statement in English: "Doctor Madam, you will please make me careful examination. I am suffering a fatal attack of ammonia."

Sometimes our hospital pictures are all sunlight and laughter.

Poshamma, the hospital cook, came one day and, gravely, but with a peculiar twinkle in her eye, asked me to come and see "a new patient."

There on the cook-house steps close by the dispensary door sat an enormous gray monkey with black face and tail-tip, eating leisurely and with evident enjoyment some bread which kind-hearted Poshamma had given him, his self-satisfied expression showing plainly that he realized his descent from the intrepid builders of Rama's bridge.

XXXII

YOUNG HOPEFULS

ALMOST as interesting to me as the hospital were the schools for boys and girls. When I came to Medak, I could scarcely credit the information that the filthy, ignorant coolie men and women of the compound were the parents of the neat, intelligent lads and lassies in the schools. These coolies, as might be expected from a race subject for centuries, and with a religion having no connection with morality, are born liars and thieves, and, worse, unashamed of their shortcomings.

Knowing this fact, I was surprised one day to hear the schoolgirl daughter of a coolie say, with a proud toss of her head and a flash of her eyes: "Do you think I would lie? No, indeed! A lie is not only wicked but is silly and cowardly!" Possibly the little miss may not be able to live up to her ideals at all times—thus differing in no wise from the rest of us mortals—but I loved her for the pride of her tone and for the hope she represented.

The poorest of our Western school children would feel a deep pity for these little folk whose life is a study in simplicity, their bed, a blanket on a wooden floor; their chair and table, another wooden floor; their dress, two thin garments; and their food, rice and chilis. The pity of the Western children would be wasted, however, for frequently what we Westerners consider the necessaries of life are regarded as oppressive burdens by these people.

Our little folk find much to make them happy. They are happier still when a wedding is in progress, and happiest of all when the wedding is a double wedding, such as took place during my first year at Medak. The brides, garlanded with flowers, and with faces modestly drooping, were charming in white *saris* and yellow and green satin jackets and skirts, while the bridegrooms, in white muslin with gay, colored scarfs draped over the left shoulder, and also wearing garlands of flowers, presented a dignified, manly appearance. After the service, powdered spices were thrown by the jovially disposed guests into the eyes of the brides and grooms, and they were showered with rice as they climbed into the bullock *tonga,* which was conducted with great rejoicing all about the compound, the shouts and laughter every now and then giving place to the loud and ringing wedding song, *Tsahla Santo-shamoo!* (Great Joy.)

Durganna, formerly a Dacoitie boy, is one of our big band of schoolboys. The Dacoities are born to the occupation of robbery and murder, but they have a social standing and are as proud of their work as any Brahman. When one realizes that they are trained to all the steps of deceit and crime as soon as their baby brains will grasp connected thoughts, one feels only pity for the victims of this evil system. After all, the Dacoities are not entirely different from the rest of the mild-mannered, affectionate Indian people.

A tall, pleasant-faced lad used to lie at my feet in the evening and, by the light of my punkah-lamp, slowly trace with his fingers the Telugu characters in his reading-book. Every little while he would look up and ask me some question about what he was reading. This was Durganna. From his birth he had been trained in all the wicked arts of the Dacoities, but when he was yet a child his father was convicted of a crime and imprisoned. This was during the terrible famine of '96 and '97, and Durganna and his mother, in despair, sought work at the Christian "Famine Camp." Durganna became an errand boy and slowly but surely the evil of

Boys' playground, Medak

Girls' playground, Medak

his education was supplanted by good and he became a Christian, ambitious to be an evangelist. Long and hard he worked at his first reading-book, and then at all the books that followed, until his triumph came when he brilliantly passed his entrance examinations for the theological training school.

Dina was a mite of a girl who was worse than motherless. For a few rupees which had been offered her by a Mahomedan *zenana,* the mother consented to sell Dina as a slave if she could but steal her from the school. This we intended to prevent, if possible, for, when our Mission took Dina, her mother signed papers forfeiting all her rights in the child.

One day Dina seemed very much frightened and for several days thereafter kept close to Miss Richardson, her school-superintendent, of whom she was very fond. At last she confided the cause of her terror.

"My mother came again in the night," she whispered in awed tones. "Always before, she has offered me sweetmeats if I would run away with her, but I told her I loved you too well to leave you. This time she was very cross with me, and when she went away she said she would come again some night and choke me to death unless I would go with her, but I didn't go!"

However, we watched Dina very carefully, and after several months her mother gave up her fruitless attempts to steal her.

Our Jesumani (Jewel of Jesus), a young Bible woman and the bride of one of our leading evangelists, was but three years of age when she was dedicated by her parents, in return for a valuable piece of land and a yearly offering of rice, to the life of a devil priestess, a life almost too revolting for description. She was ten years old when the Mission found her. Her long, uncombed, unwashed hair and the bits of leather tied about her neck told of the life of shame before her, and, according to custom, her parents were making ready to offer her as a sacrifice to her profession. This meant that, during a drunken revelry of the villagers, the child would herself be made drunk and given over to the sensual brutality of the devil priest. After that she would become the common property of all unscrupulous men. However, obtaining support for the child and for her family, also, as she was their mainstay, and overcoming all the stubborn opposition that bigotry and hatred of foreign intrusion could present, the Mission set her free. To-day, looking at Jesumani's happy face, it would be hard to realize that she confronted but a few years ago the most horrible fate that could befall a woman.

Nerickshanna, another of our schoolgirls, was always a brave Christian soldier. A schoolmate starting home for vacation placed on her forehead—thoughtless vanity her probable motive—a dot of vermilion, which is a sign of Hinduism. Nerickshanna spied the mark and rubbed it off with no gentle hand.

"How dare you," she exclaimed indignantly, "adorn yourself with the sign of the heathen gods and thus disgrace our Lord Jesus!"

Nerickshanna had an excellent memory, and often attempted to sing English songs she had heard (the child did not understand one word of English). Her favorite was "Little Alabama Coon," and she got the melody perfectly, singing lustily and with confidence:

> Go to seep, my lily pipanimbo,
> Unnerneaf ee siller, suller moon.

She was in hospital with malaria when a baby born to one of the patients died before it had ever breathed. In her prayer that evening Nerickshanna pleaded with tears in her eyes: "O God, the baby that died to-day was never baptized, so I suppose it is in hell; but wherever it is, dear God, please bless and take care of the sweet little baby!"

A seven-year-old schoolboy fell from a high swing and broke his arm. An honest fraud was this same schoolboy. I allowed him to come into my room one day to play with the chessmen. When he went away I examined his arm to see if it were improving, and out from the sling dropped two of the knights.

"Oh, my dear," I exclaimed, "how could you steal from me? Have I not always been good to you?"

His large eyes grew larger with injured innocence.

"I stole them not," he protested, "they accrued to me from that game I was playing!"

Then and there I took the boy's morals in hand and talked to him for five minutes for his soul's good. I had expected, at the end of my eloquent harangue, tears and repentance, but he gravely inquired: "If I had asked you for the little figures, would you have given them to me?"

"No," I replied. "They are part of an expensive game."

"Then," he concluded, clinching his argument, "if I had not taken them without permission, how else could I have obtained them?"

XXXIII

PENETRATING THE WILDS

ANOTHER tour, "penetrating the wilds!" It was late afternoon when we started out into unknown regions, unknown to our *tonga* driver as well as to ourselves, and more especially unknown to our "guide." In spite of our slight anxiety at the thought of a moonless, starless, dinnerless, blanketless night in the jungle, and of the fact that jolting over the rough roads had made us all "sorry in the stomach," as little Eva Adkin used to express it, we could not suppress our amusement at the guide's directions, our driver in bewilderment turning this way and that, retracing the path over and over, until we hysterically told him to ignore the statements of that will o' the wisp guide and to go straight ahead.

At last, late at night, far away on a hill top, a light gleamed, and in glad relief we felt that people must be there who could give us an idea of our whereabouts. On reaching the light, what was our surprise and joy to find it our own lantern shining from the tent which had gone on ahead with the servants! A delicious chicken curry and a steaming cup of tea soon compensated us for all our troubles.

In the morning we were awakened by a woman's loud wailing near the tent, and we learned that a fourteen-year-old wife had been severely beaten by her husband and was lying prostrate on the ground just outside. While we soothed her with words and medicine, we could but compare this with an incident of the day before—the beginning of a Lombardy honeymoon! On rounding a turn, we had seen a white bullock decked out, Lombardy fashion, with shreds of cloth of various gaudy colors and with bits of shell and looking-glass dangling over his forehead, surrounding his horns, and fluttering in the breeze. Just behind came a handsome, stalwart Lombardy holding close, in a vain endeavor to comfort her, his young bride who was wailing bitterly as, in her new rainbow suit, with her thick blanket hiding her face, she left the shelter of her parents' home for that of her husband. Far off on the road above her, the family group waved their good-bye, the mother wailing as the daughter wailed, the more philosophic old grandmother bending over the mother as if speaking words of wisdom and comfort. As we

Medak doctor on tour

Medak nurse visiting the sick in a palanquin

passed, the bride's curiosity got the better of her grief and she took her blanket from her face and stopped crying to have a good look at us.

On our march to the second village, the roughest of roads compelled us to walk miles in the noonday sun, and we all came off with sore feet and sun headaches. The baggage cart twice overturned, breaking our tapestrung bed and injuring the driver. However, we managed to get at least a thin layer of straw on which to sleep for the next few nights, and the driver's wounds soon healed.

It was on this trip that we saw three large mango trees just beside the road, swarming with thousands of flying foxes. We were indeed glad to exchange the deafening noise—rustling, squeaking, squealing—and the suffocating vermin-odor for the breezes sweeping across the rippling blue of the great lake by which we camped. It was a wild jungle spot, and the inhabitants of the neighboring village were terrified by the bold visits of tigers or leopards which struck down sheep and goats by the score. The savage creatures had left the remains of a few of their victims close by our camp, and it took some time to remove them. During that first afternoon, while the servants were cleaning the ground for the tent, they killed three venomous snakes.

"Abo!" exclaimed our evangelist. "That is a very bad sign; if patients see, they would not come!"

Distemper, too, had wrought havoc among the cows and goats, so, according to custom, a small boy led a sheep up and down before it should be sacrificed to Siva in an appeal for mercy.

Certainly this little village seemed in sad disfavor of its gods. At night so fierce a storm broke over us, that with all our strength we could scarcely hold up the tent poles, firmly fixed in the ground as they were; and it was early morning before the strength of the gale subsided and we could lie down to sleep. Even then we were disturbed by the coolies loudly shouting and waving lights to scare away the leopards.

On the first day at this village the *patel* lent us his gracious countenance for nine consecutive hours. As he watched the patients crowd forward with their various ailments he noted carefully each new disease, and as we gave the medicine for it he would gravely tell us that some one of his household had this same disease and he would like medicine to cure it, until he had a sample—a very small one, you may be sure—of nearly everything in stock.

As we returned to the tent, after an evening stroll, the servants told us that a cobra which had been killed in a village house had been brought for us to see. To catch the reptile a man had baited a strong hook with a toad, and when the snake, from its underground fastnesses, seized the bait, the man quickly jerked it forth to its death with the hook through its jaw. I gave the man a present and kept the snake for its skin. After holding an interesting autopsy over the creature, which measured six feet in length and five inches in circumference, we delivered the skin to our "boy" for preservation.

A weird scene that night was the worship about an anthill. Once some god or other had been buried in an anthill, so now, in memoriam, on a certain day of the year, crowds of men bury a bit of molded clay in an anthill to represent the dead god and then march round and round the anthill carrying lighted torches and wailing loudly for the dead.

About dawn next morning, we heard a rustle of the straw under our cots. Thinking that a pariah dog had found its way into the tent, we called the butler to come and drive it forth, when what was our surprise to see a tall, haggard man slowly emerge from beneath the cot. Gazing wildly at us for a moment, he gave a piercing shriek and darted from the tent. Later we learned his story.

He was a rich, high caste Hindu merchant whom domestic unhappiness had driven mad. There is no confinement in India of "the dead who walk," as they call the insane, and this unfortunate lunatic roamed about at will. Our people gave him food and otherwise treated him kindly; so, throughout our stay at his village, he remained close by the tents, watching our every movement. We took care, however, that he did not again sleep beneath our bed.

When we drove on to Dhoomkonda, the mad merchant ran and leaped and danced beside us all the way. Now and then, with a shrill scream, he would dash past the *tonga* at full speed, holding his head in his hands; then he would pause and quietly smoke as he walked beside us, depositing matches or rice or flowers at our feet. It was all very pathetic!

Dhoomkonda is ruled by a rajah and is very strong in its caste prejudices. There is not a single Christian in all that large town. However, the people crowded upon us thickly, as usual. Five hundred and forty-six patients received treatment the first day. Our poor *cha-*

prassi, in his attempt to hold back the throng, was seized roughly by a big Mahomedan who tore to shreds the *chaprassi's* pink turban, his pride and joy. This insult was too much, and, in spite of belonging to a Christian camp, the *chaprassi* engaged in a free fight then and there, which required much effort on our part to stay.

In one of the villages we visited the people had never before seen a white face, and when we started out for a stroll they followed us respectfully but with unveiled curiosity. We at last sat down beneath a tree and called the people to come and talk to us. As they timidly drew near one of the men, looking at our shoes, exclaimed: "How strange you people are! You have white faces and black feet with no toes, and we know not whether you be men or women. Your features are like a woman's, but you hold your heads up and walk quickly and proudly as no woman would walk!"

We were delighted to find here and there in our travels patients who had been treated by us before and who were loud in their gratitude. One, a Brahman girl who had been cured in our hospital, proudly showed us her garden.

"See," she said, as she pointed to a tree or a flower, "I saw them in the garden at your hospital; when I came home I straightway planted the same kind in my own garden."

While in hospital, this young Brahman girl, Parvatiamma, had won our hearts by her sweet disposition and patience under suffering. For years she had borne this pain which was destroying all her joy in life. After coming to us, a very simple treatment had restored her health, but she could scarcely realize that she was cured. Her mother, an old Brahman widow with a keen sense of humor, said one day: "See my daughter's face, see it! She is waiting for the pain and it will not come." Then she laughed joyously and the daughter laughed with her.

At the same time that the Brahman girl, Parvatiamma, was in the hospital, Sangamma, a Hindu low caste girl, was there also. Sangamma was a child-woman of sixteen, so thin and frail that our hearts ached for her. Her husband had deserted her for a stronger wife; her mother was dead; but the fond old father regularly brought her food and begged us to care for her and to make her well.

"When she is well I will give you a rupee!" he said grandly, and his chest swelled with pride at the munificence of his promise.

Sangamma got into trouble one day by unwittingly touching Parvatiamma's dress. The wrath of the Brahman was heavy on the head of the low caste girl, and there was much bathing and purifying in the wards. Sangamma, trembling with fear, promised to be careful in future, but her apologies seemed not to soften the wrath of the defiled Brahman. A few days later, as I sat by Parvatiamma's bed talking to her, she drew my head down to hers and whispered: "I shall aways be a Brahman, but I should like to be an unselfish Brahman, as you white people are unselfish Christians."

When I made my rounds that evening, I heard little Sangamma crying weakly in her corner, for the day had been more trying than usual for her. As I started toward her to comfort her, I stopped amazed. Not seeing me behind her, Parvatiamma who, less than a week before, had cursed Sangamma because their garments had accidentally come into contact, bent over the weeping child and, stroking her cheek, said gently: "Cry not, little one! Courage, dear! The pain will soon go and you will again be happy."

To those who know not India, this physical touching by a Brahman of one lower in caste may seem a slight thing, but I, understanding what it meant in loving self-sacrifice, felt too deeply touched for words and stole silently out of the ward.

And now Parvatiamma showed us her pretty garden. She declared she was "as happy as a bulbul," and when we said good-bye to her she showered us with blessings and loaded us with gifts. In gay procession, we passed through the streets of the quaint old town with its crumbling wall, our people following close after us, the "boy" in advance of the rest and bearing on his head an enormous plate of sugar, cocoanuts and oranges; then the two nurses in costumes of crimson and orange and rose pink, and the vast majority of the villagers bringing up the rear.

As we turned our faces toward Medak, we stopped at a village where we had toured three years before. At that time we were asked to visit a woman "with a marble in her breast." She was a Brahman, so she did not invite us to enter her house, but came to us on the outer veranda. I found upon examination that the "marble" was a cancer, and I explained fully the danger and the necessity for immediate operation. Months passed, and then came Brahman Lakshmamma to our hospital. The "marble" had grown to a hideous sore, and she had at last decided to submit herself to our hands.

"We have tried every other doctor and every

remedy known to us," said her three grown sons, prostrating themselves at my feet, "but all have failed; now in perfect faith we come to you!"

I performed the operation and Lakshmamma made a good recovery and went home. This time, when we came to her village, Lakshmamma herself met us far down the street and drew us into her house and into the courtyard close to her sacred Tulsi plant and to the shrine of her household god. Smilingly she beckoned to our nurses and assistants to follow, and then whispered something to her eldest son. He hastily left us and in a few minutes returned with all the Brahmans in the village at his heels.

"I have invited them," said Lakshmamma, "to hear the sweet music of your Telugu Christian hymns which I heard with such delight while in your hospital."

Several hymns were sung, the people listening in silent pleasure. Then Lakshmamma turned to Abbishakamma:

"Now will you tell us the story of Elizabeth?" she requested. "It is good for these young women to hear."

The dusk had settled over the landscape before we finally departed for our long trip home, with garlands about our necks and Lakshmamma's blessing in our ears.

As next morning we drove through a thick woodland, we saw, strutting in the underbrush, a peacock, his beautiful feathers gleaming in the sunshine, and by his side his meek little hen and five baby chicks.

XXXIV

FANTASTIC SUMMER'S HEAT

WHEN, during my last year at Medak, the hot April sun made us all long for "the Hills," I decided to resist the temptation to go, keeping my money for an extensive sightseeing trip on my way home to America. Hotter and hotter blazed the sun as the days dragged by, and the fitful breezes might have been from the depths of a furnace fire. All nature looked like a man burning with high fever. The *maidan* was dried to a yellow-brown shade; the pipal trees held up to the sun rigid skeleton arms pleading for mercy; the air shimmered with the intensity of the heat; the birds sat with wings outstretched and with beaks open, gasping for air; while not a sound broke the stillness except the lazy drone of the bees. On the damp floor of the bathroom our pet terriers found their only approach to comfort, hugging close the water pots and panting breathlessly. For myself, I tried to keep cool by thinking of May in the home country, its spring green of new grass, the violets and anemones scattering their beauty through the woods, and the apple blossoms crowning the orchards with purity and sweetness. I tried to imagine the exhilarating air and the song of the nesting birds. Often it was too hot even for this, and my bursting head held only a dull longing that the day would end.

Fortunately, people were too hot to realize they were sick, or else too hot to come for medicine when they were sick, so I had leisure to sit beneath the waving *punkah* and feel the pleasant stirring of the hot air.

Then came Miss Hare, a Secunderabad missionary, with some of her school children; Mr. Johnson and Mr. Adkin, two of our Medak missionaries, returned from a tour in the outer district, and, all working together to help the little folks enjoy their vacation, we managed to have a very pleasant summer.

Every nurse and servant tried to outdo every other in loving service to us, and through all the weary summer weeks their zeal and loyalty never flagged.

The gramophone, mango feasts, especially elaborate dinners on the flat roof of the hospital, magic lantern stories, picnics at the old hill-fort and on the beautiful Huldi River, and various other festivities, kept us all busy in preparation and enjoyment.

To add to the pleasure and excitement, the Yellaka people came one evening to visit us. The Yellaka people are a nomadic tribe of gypsy fortune tellers, black-skinned, keen-witted, cheerful hearted, and clothed in uniform of Kipling's *Gunga Din,* who drive from village to village cattle and donkeys which, with baskets they have woven, and with other merchandise, they sell and thus earn a livelihood. The Telugu peasants generally have harsh, unmodulated voices, but I have rarely heard voices softer or more musical than the Yellakas'. One bright-eyed young woman begged me to have my fortune told, so I obediently seated myself on the grass and listened, more to the sweetness of the voice that spoke than to the matter spoken. Weaving her body to and fro, she placed my hand which she held on her forehead, then on my own forehead, and murmured on and on for several minutes, until she had convinced me that at least she had a clear brain and a remarkable power of deduction. Then, at our request, the whole band of gypsies gave us an exhibition of their extraordinary powers of mimicry. Their jackal howl set the dogs barking furiously and darting again and again into the shadows to find the noisy disturbers of the night's peace.

When the Yellakas had finished their performance and had tied in their turbans the coins we gave them, they begged to hear the "man machine" (gramophone) of which they had heard. We turned on a Telugu song or two which they greatly enjoyed. Then we gave them the "Laughing Song," and the peals of laughter from the gramophone set the queer black folk rolling on the ground in uncontrolled mirth.

So one hot day quickly succeeded another, and the cool winds of June were blowing up from Ceylon, telling that the monsoon had broken, before we realized that vacation was ended and life was about to resume its ordinary routine.

XXXV

STRENUOUS TIMES

ONE afternoon messengers came to us in deep distress, begging us to go with them and give treatment to a "sick child" at a village "only eight miles distant, over good roads." I was very busy at the hospital and feared to leave some of the patients, but the messengers said that the parents of the child were especially orthodox Hindus, who would not bring him to a Christian hospital; that the child had been sick but a few days and had had no other treatment; and that now surely when they had become anxious about him, we would respect their faith in us shown by not calling in *hakims,* and would come at once. At last their piteous appeals won me and I started forth in the *tonga* with one of the English ladies who insisted on accompanying me, and with our *chaprassi,* fully armed.

Of all rough rides I have taken in rough-roaded India that ride was the roughest. Often the *tonga* dropped straight down two feet into a gutter; often to help the bullocks in their impossible task we dismounted and pushed the *tonga;* often we climbed out and walked through the ankle-deep mud of the rice fields; until, late at night, footsore and exhausted, we arrived at our journey's end with the knowledge that the messengers had lied to us about the distance as well as about the condition of the roads; that instead of eight the village was twenty miles from Medak. The sick "child" proved to be thirty years old, and the son of the *patel.* We learned then that his people feared we would not come should they tell us the truth, as our hospital is known to be especially for women and children.

A hasty examination showed me that the patient had but a short time to live, and I called his father and younger brother aside, saying: "He is dying; I cannot help him."

Prostrating themselves at my feet, they begged me to do "something—anything."

"If you do not give him medicine the women will know that he is dying and will wail; then he will know and be frightened."

"Very well," said I, "all you people of India know what brandy is; I will give him a little brandy."

Leaning over the young man, I poured a large spoonful of diluted brandy down his throat.

Immediately he cried out in agony: "Oh, the burning, the burning!" and I realized that the *hakims* had ruined the patient's stomach by their drastic concoctions. He was dying fast now, so, pushing my way through the crowd which had gathered, I sat down with my English friend on a ruined stone foundation of a house, raised above the level of the street, and there we awaited the end as the father had begged us to do, fearing our departure would tell the sad truth to the patient and to his women relatives.

In about an hour the sudden, loud wail told us the man had died, and a moment later our *chaprassi,* with ashen face and eyes starting from their sockets, ran toward us.

"They say you have killed him," he gasped, "and that they will kill you to avenge him; they are furious with the fury of a tiger; let us run!"

At his heels came the mob. As far as I could see, men and women with angry faces and with threatening cries and gestures rushed toward us, their voices rising louder and louder in fierce condemnation, till the sound was like the gathering of a thunder storm.

"Run!" I echoed scornfully—I was too indignant to feel afraid—"I will never run from the cowardly dogs!" With my English friend standing at my side, and with the *chaprassi*—valiant fellow!—cowering behind me, I rose to my full height on the platform of stone, and, facing the mob, held up my hand in a gesture demanding silence.

Surprised into stillness by my attitude, they stopped.

Then, in my best Telugu, and marveling at the fluency excitement had given me, I began:

"Men and women, listen to my words and tell me are you treating me fairly?

"You lied to me when you said the patient was a child; you lied to me when you said he had been ill but a few days, and had taken no other medicine but mine; now you admit that this is the end of weeks of illness; you admit that you have given the medicines of every *hakim* that would come. You told me your village was eight miles distant from Medak; it is twenty, and we traveled rough roads to reach you. When I came I told the patient's own father and brother that he was dying; that I could do nothing to help him; and only at their earnest request, and against my own wish, did I give him medicine (I explained to them what medicine I had given). Now you say I murdered him. Is your accusation just? Is the man's death any benefit to me? No. Then why should I murder him? On the contrary, should I not have done all I could to save his life, and thus win the friendship of your village, which you know to be the desire of our Mission? Stand forth!" I concluded, pointing my finger at the father and brother of the patient, "and show yourselves to be men! Tell these people I have spoken truly!"

I stopped and, amid the buzzing voices which followed my protest, I heard the clear tones of the dead man's father. "Yes, truly she has spoken. We are in the wrong," and one by one the people of the great crowd slunk back to their dead, leaving us to go our way in peace.

Then, only, did I feel the nervous strain. For a moment everything swam before me, and it was a mighty effort that gave me strength enough to climb into the *tonga,* where I sank down almost unconscious.

Traveling on through the jungle, we stopped toward daylight under a big tree and slept for an hour and a half. Then we bathed our faces in the river, had some tea and bread from the tiffin basket, and pushed along. It was literally "pushing along," too, for, as we climbed the hill toward home, our *chaprassi* mysteriously disappeared. We learned afterward that he had been overcome with cholera, but had managed to stagger home—and we three, now without the help of the *chaprassi's* strong arm, had to push the heavy *tonga* up the fearful ruts and gaps in the road, too much for the strength of the bulls alone, until, with sun headaches and a pessimistic view of life in general, we reached the compound.

The *chaprassi* recovered from the cholera, which he always said was brought on by his fright at the mob.

Other excitements were in store for us.

Even in this India of glorious nights I am sure that night when five of us missionaries, accompanied by Rajah and Rani, our pet fox-terriers, had set out on a tour to Ramyanpett was the most glorious, the most weirdly enchanting. The trees and underbrush on both sides of the lonely jungle road glistened with myriads of fireflies until it was impossible to tell where those glowing, twinkling stars of earth joined the glowing, twinkling stars of heaven. In the midst shone Venus like a radiant young moon. The warm air was heavy with the scent of lemon- and spice-grasses; the jackals and the giant frogs held high carnival; and, through the shrill howls and hoarse croaks, came startling at intervals the mournful hoot of an owl.

We had tired of the *tonga* and had climbed down to eat supper by the light of a lantern, on a flat, roadside rock. As we ate and laughed and chatted, we recalled that it was just about at the spot where we were sitting that leopards had frequently been seen, and that a tiger had, a few days before, killed the horse of the *Zemindar.* This did not lessen our appetites, but we spoke again of these things as, supper finished, we strolled along in the road following the *tonga,* the terriers trotting about thirty yards behind us. Suddenly Rani uttered a sharp cry, and we turned quickly. There was a loud crash of bushes as a heavy body bounded away among the rocks, and our little dog had disappeared never to be seen again. Though we were unarmed, we felt no fear for ourselves. Nevertheless, we could not help a "creepy" sensation when we thought of how long the savage beast must have stalked us before it dared spring so boldly on our unfortunate pet.

After Rani's death, Rajah never recovered his good spirits. Instead of the playful, affectionate little dog he had been, he became quiet and morose, shrinking into corners and frequently refusing his food. We thought him pining for his playmate, but we were finally forced to the conclusion that his condition was more serious than that. Miss Tombleson, returning from Ramyanpett, reported that Rajah, who had gone with her, had, quite contrary to his usual conduct, sprung suddenly on a pariah dog and bitten it savagely;

Miss Tombleson had pulled him away, and, for the first time in his life, he had turned on her and bitten her hand, drawing the blood.

After they came home that night, I was alone in my room, Rajah lying quietly at my feet, when Jack, a fox-terrier belonging to Miss Beaulah, one of our English ladies, came running in. Like a flash, Rajah sprang upon him. I seized a desk ruler lying near, and, jerking the smaller dog from Rajah's grasp, gave Rajah a sharp blow with the ruler. Instantly he turned, and, with a low growl, sprang straight at my throat. As he sprang, I dodged, and that second the truth came to me. Rajah had gone mad. Then suddenly I recalled the words of an animal trainer whose performance I had seen in my childhood: "'It 'em in the nose w'en they gets savage! That's w'ere you've got 'em—in the nose!"

Again and again, with bloodshot eyes, bristling hair and foaming mouth, the dog sprang at me. At each spring I met him with a sharp rap on the nose, until at last he crouched low in a corner apparently subdued. I backed from the room and, closing the door, ran to call a servant. The dog made no resistance as we tied a rope about his neck and made him fast, meaning to decide his fate by a morning consultation.

Long after midnight, our Miss Beaulah was

awakened by the sound of some animal leaping over the lower half of her door, and she jumped out of bed just in time to see Rajah viciously assail little Jack, the terrier, who was tied in a corner. Miss Beaulah had been half ill for several days, and to beat Rajah off her pet with a chair and finally from the room was a task almost beyond her strength, and left her prostrated with fright and exhaustion. When daylight came, Rajah was discovered cowering in a corner of our veranda, wild-eyed, covered with blood, and every few minutes giving the single, sharp bark, shrill and pitiful, of rabies. The rope with which we had tied him was gnawed in two and a dead pariah dog, terribly mangled, found in the garden, explained Rajah's bloody coat. There could be no more delay. Miss Tombleson consented to have her pet shot, and, sad at heart, we walked out over the *maidan* to be away from the tragedy. We had walked scarcely two miles when a rifle shot rang out, and we knew our little Rajah had joined his playmate Rani.

The conviction that Rajah's illness was rabies brought the knowledge that Miss Tombleson ran the risk of contracting the disease from the wound he had given her, so I sent her at once to Coonoor, where was the nearest Pasteur Institute, and she has suffered no ill effects from Rajah's bite.

A few weeks later came the rainy season.

Heavily, steadily for days the rain poured down, swelling the brooks to rivers and the rivers to seas.

The rainy season in India is called—very appropriately that last year—the "sick season." Our hospital was crowded to the doors, and many of our patients were in rough temporary shelters of straw. The number treated at the dispensary was enormous; and almost everybody that was not actually sick felt damp and miserable.

It was during this time that Miss Tombleson and I went to Ramyanpett to give out some necessary medicines. We forded with difficulty the two streams that brawled across the road and next day, when we wished to return to Medak, the *bandy* driver told us the streams had swollen so greatly during the night that we should probably not be able to cross. However, we felt that we must, if possible, get back to the hospital, and we boldly set forth, while the rain rained on, the wettest, wettest rain!

Arriving at the first stream, we saw that fording it would be dangerous for the bullocks, so we told Latchman to put them up in the rest house, and we would try to walk home by ourselves.

Along the bank in the tall, wet grass we stumbled, trying to find some crossing point and at last, telling Miss Tombleson to wait on the bank, I plunged in. Though the water was but waist deep, I could scarcely stand against the rushing flood. Suddenly I sank to my neck, and in an instant was being whirled down stream powerless to resist. Fortunately a branch of a tree projected over the water. This I seized and, holding it with all my might, for I knew it meant life itself, I managed to drag myself to the bank. The noise of the wind and the waters drowned Miss Tombleson's voice, but I could see her face blanched with terror, and the look of relief when, somewhat bruised and scratched, I climbed up and rejoined her.

With a little more caution, we tried to cross the stream at several other points, but failed. At last, to our joy, we found a wide, shallow place where the water was comparatively quiet, and succeeded in crossing over.

What was our surprise to find that Latchman had also crossed with the bullocks swimming, and was waiting for us.

All this had taken time, and when we came to the bank of the second stream, which was swirling as viciously as the first, we realized that it would be madness to attempt to cross it in the pitchy darkness of the night. There was nothing to do but to resign ourselves to the inevitable. Soaked to the skin, we wrapped our dripping rugs about us and, climbing into the *bandy,* sat all night on the wet cushions, now waking to the sound of the wild wind and rain and of the croaking frogs; and again, in spite of the discomfort, sleeping from pure weariness.

In the morning we perched ourselves on the back of the *bandy* seat, and, with the help of the ropes in the hands of hired coolies, were pulled across. An hour later we were at home and thankful for the cup of hot tea which the solicitous butler placed before us.

Then came the Hyderabad floods, one of the great disasters of the world, which will be long remembered by us who were eye-witnesses of the frightful devastation.

Half the entire rainfall of the year fell within less than two days. During those few short hours the Musah River, flowing through the very center of Hyderabad City, rose sixty feet, wreaking havoc indescribable. In the heart of the great city of four hundred and fifty thousand inhabitants a district one mile long and half a mile wide, containing thirty thousand residences and other buildings, was utterly destroyed. In the country beyond, whole villages were swept away, thousands of lives were lost, and millions of rupees' worth of property.

It was reported that the Nizam, on learning of the terrible loss of life, wept like a child.

Of course, such a sudden and awful calamity brought everywhere to light heroes of the bravest, many of whom must forever be unknown and unnamed. The Afzul Ganj Hospital, the public *zenana* hospital of Hyderabad City, was in the center of the ruined area. As the river overflowed its banks and climbed higher and higher, the lady nurses, two of whom were Rohillas and one a Sikh, realized the danger and, with the help of coolies, managed to convey all of their patients, except one who was dying, to safety on the roof of the Char Minar.

The Char Minar is a huge mosque with four minarets and four arches, which, before the flood, was at the center of the business district of Hyderabad, and under whose arches ran four of the largest streets of the city. On its high flat roof the Afzul Ganj nurses and their charges found refuge and there, all that cold night, they sat, clad in night dresses or dressing gowns, trying to protect their patients from the pouring rain. In the morning they were found by the lady doctors of the hospital, who lived in the outskirts of the city, and who had many times risked their lives on reeling, falling bridges before they finally reached the Char Minar, and had their nurses and patients taken in boats to a more comfortable refuge.

Miss Tombleson and I, in a visit to Hyderabad three weeks later to see the ruins, found the whole country still a vast lake. The ruins themselves, miles of wrecked buildings, spoke of horrible things in a language plainer than words.

XXXVI

THE CHOLERA TERROR

WHILE these sorrows and anxieties were filling our hearts, the cholera terror crept insidiously into the Medak District, and swift and terrible was the slaughter of its victims. Families, streets, villages of people were wiped out of existence. Along every highway, at frequent intervals, was stretched across the road from tree to tree the rope of mango leaves which implores Misamma, the devil goddess of cholera, not to go farther. Little mud temples painted with the sacred red and yellow stripes, and heaped with offerings of wild flowers and rice and milk, were erected here and there by the wayside, and prayers by the thousands were made to the goddess of cholera, begging mercy. Life was one long nightmare. Continually, day and night, we could hear the loud wailing of mourners for their dead; and, one following close on the heels of the other, went the sad processions, wending their way to funeral pyre or burial ground.

One of these processions appeared so extraordinary that I could hardly believe the man they mourned was dead. Wrapped in an orange colored cloth and supported by two other men, the dead man sat upright in a country cart, which was followed by a long stream of people chanting mournfully. It was a Lingyat funeral. The corpse is buried in this sitting posture in a niche built in one side of a large grave.

By stationing guards at every gate, and by rigid rules concerning those coming and going, we kept the cholera from the people of our compound, although outside cases were received through the hospital entrance and placed in temporary, isolated shacks under the charge and treatment of our hospital. Frequently a hundred and fifty cases at once were under our care, and our regular nurses and as many other people as we could press into the service were nearly exhausted with work and worry.

One case only broke out among the Christians. Our dear Monikyam was just sixteen, and on the eve of her marriage, when the cholera poison entered her fragile body, which had never recovered from the privations she had suffered during the famine of '99. I was roused one night by the cry: "Monikyam is very ill!" Always prepared during those weeks for instant response to the frequent night calls, I was almost immediately at the girl's bedside. Even then she was beyond all earthly help, but to the last she was, as she had always been, wholly unselfish. I had been working for a few minutes over her almost unconscious form when she whispered weakly: "Do lie down, Doctor, dear; you will be so tired; I am not very sick; I shall be quite well in the morning."

The little hand, wrinkled like an old woman's from the wasting disease, weakly stroked my face as the eyelids closed over the eyes sunk deep in the hollowed cheeks. We had already sent for her family, and by the utmost effort I managed to keep her with us until her people reached her side and received a last smiling gleam of recognition before she passed "beyond the Gates."

I would that some of those who scoff at "first generation Christians" could see the white pages of Monikyam's life since, as a little child, she, with all her family, accepted Christ.

As the cholera epidemic began slowly to lessen, the cunning priests, according to their wont, added more silver to their ill-gotten gains through the great "Sacrifice of Gaoo," by which they pretend to win mercy from the cholera goddess.

Under ordinary circumstances Christians would be excluded from witnessing the Gaoo sacrifice, but our superintendent had been kind to the devil priests in many ways, so we were allowed to be present and to take photographs.

The first day was devoted to preliminary rites: A great, rainbow-colored rabble of men, women and children, such as can be seen only in the East, filthy and scant of clothing, filthy and by no means scant of speech, crowd close to the narrow, cleared space where the *poojah* is to be held. A sheep is slaughtered and a devil priestess, her long, tangled hair floating over her shoulders, smears herself with the blood and dips her garment in the red flow from the throat. Then, winding the animal's intestines around her neck and holding the dripping heart in her mouth, she proceeds to go into various semblances of the "prophet's trance," trembling, fainting, staring. Meanwhile her assistants beat loudly on drums and scatter leaves upon her until, waving a rice basket over her head, she breaks forth in a wailing voice,

"The Devil requires many human lives tomorrow, as many as there are grains of rice in this basket!"

In a frenzy of desperation the people rush toward the loathsome creature and, laying at her feet rupees, sheep, goats, fowls, rice, beg for her intercession with the cruel cholera devil.

On the second day the sacrifice reaches the height—or the depths—of degradation.

All the ground has been carefully swept and decorated with various geometrical patterns in colored chalk. Just in front of the little temple at one end is a row of sheeps' heads, and in front of these again a great heap of sheeps' meat and bones. Near this, and almost too small for observation, stand a spinning wheel and other household utensils, toilet articles, toy servants, a palanquin, a wooden elephant, and several tiny wooden horses harnessed to a Juggernaut car, covered by a red silk canopy; all for the use of Misamma, the cholera goddess.

Beyond a large, bare space for the pouring of libations lies a row of buffaloes' heads, each with a piece of skin removed from brow to nose, with one of its own severed legs in its mouth, and on its forehead a small, earthen lamp alight. Still beyond, under a shelter of sacred leaves, is a heap of cooked meat and rice, beside which rest two earthen vessels filled with toddy, sacred leaves twined about the neck of each vessel. Little native lamps burn here and there with a vile smell of cheap oil and smoke; while at the end of the space opposite the temple stands the principal figure, the devil priestess, her hair flowing down her back and an abstracted look in her eyes, playing on a stringed instrument and accompanying herself in a low, monotonous chant as she "communes with the cholera devil."

Seventy gallons of toddy have been poured upon the ground before us, and with this and with the sacrificed animals the priestess begs the devil to be satisfied and to go away, as the people have given all they can. The devil, however, proves obdurate, and with a cry, "She is not yet satisfied!" the priestess pretends to die.

At this the people are greatly excited, and there ensues a perfect pandemonium of shouting, beating of drums, and clashing of cymbals, while sacred leaves and dust are showered about and two fowls are killed and thrown into the air. Nevertheless, not until the sacrifice amounts to fifty black-horned buffaloes, two hundred sheep, three hundred chickens, one hundred and twenty-five gallons of toddy, and many bushel basketfuls of cooked food of all sorts does the priestess return to life telling the people that at last all is well, and the devil has mounted the little Juggernaut car drawn by the wooden horses and has driven off. The fact that the car and horses remain quite stationary in the place where they have stood all day makes no impression whatever on these credulous folk.

Now, at last, comes the great event of the day.

A wild-looking old man, clad only in a loin cloth, runs up and down in the space before us, a huge whip hanging over his shoulder, till two or three men catch him and smear him thoroughly with red and yellow paste and powder making him indeed a hideous sight; then smoking incense is passed under his nose and, his toilet completed, he dashes back into view. A young man bearing a live sheep springs out of his way and a race ensues round and round the little space till at last the sheep is captured and the inhuman butchery begins. Setting his gleaming white teeth into the poor beast's lower lip, the old priest tears savagely at the quivering flesh till he reaches the jugular vein; then a fierce bite sends a warm, red stream of blood spouting into the air and ends the piteous struggles of the sheep. The priest raises his face; his features are almost blotted out with the fast clotting blood; his nostrils dilate; and his whole aspect is that of a veritable demon. He smears his whip in the blood and lashes the bystanders until they crowd back in a panic, pushing, stumbling, shrieking.

Sick and faint, I turn away and hurry unsteadily from the evil-smelling place, out into the cool air of the nearby meadows, glad indeed to realize that I am still in our own precious world of God-given joy and laughter and peace!

The disgusting Gaoo sacrifices were carried on in several other villages of the district where I was called to attend cholera patients; the gutters ran blood; and the stench of this blood and of the hundreds of dead animals was so nauseating that I could not pass through the streets. In order to visit my patients I had to climb over back fences and through pigsties.

Just such revolting work as this of the devil priest at the sacrifice of Gaoo would have fallen to our Jesu Rajahdass had he not been rescued by the Mission. It was several years ago, when Christian Jesu Rajahdass was eight-year-old heathen Potanna and the hereditary devil priest of Surjanna, which supports one of the richest devil priesthoods in the district, that one day, much to the surprise of our teacher at Surjanna, he walked boldly into the schoolroom and said: "I wish to attend your school. I do not wish to become a Christian, but I would read and write." So he came, and proved a remarkably bright pupil, easily surpassing all the others. As this boy, Potanna, learned of Christ, he grew to love him, and one day he told his teacher of his longing to be baptized a Christian. This, however, would have been the financial ruin of his parents, for he was their sole support.

Sunday Bible Class, Medak

"I cannot break my mother's heart," he sobbed, "but I will never talk with the wicked devil!"

He was twelve years old when his mother died, the greatest obstacle thus being removed. Generous Western friends promised to support the father, so at last the son was free. Still, Mr. Posnett knew there would be a frightful uproar against us in the villages, unless some step should be taken to prevent it, so he invited forty devil priests to a three days' feast and entertainment and, after winning their confidence by his friendliness, persuaded them to give little Potanna a peaceable release from his inheritance.

When the day of Potanna's baptism arrived, the chapel was packed to the doors. As the young hero stood before us making confession of his faith, there were few dry eyes among us.

One of the signs of the devil priesthood is the unkempt hair; for the hair of the devil priest is never cut or combed or washed from birth, and when Potanna took off his turban in the chapel, his dirty, matted locks fell to his knees. Mr. Posnett stood with a pair of shears in his hand and, as he picked up a strand of the hair, he asked:

"Are you sure you wish to part with this? You know it means all your worldly wealth. This act of yours can never be undone."

But the boy cried out:

"My hair may be Satan's, but my heart is Christ's! Please cut off the hair!"

He was baptized "Jesu Rajahdass" (The Slave of King Jesus), and our brave lad has always proved true to his name.

XXXVII

FAREWELLS

THE year drew to a close, and with it my Indian life.

Amid tearful prayers for my well-being from nurses and patients, I parted from my hospital; and on the last night a service was held for me in the chapel, when all the people in the compound, English and Indian, gathered together to wish me godspeed. The beautiful gift in which they all joined, and the words of affection and gratitude and good will, made me almost powerless to steady my voice as, with those hundreds of gentle, loving faces before me, I rose to say good-by.

Christmas Day found me traveling southward, and a day later I was in the Tamil country—real Hindu land—where everybody and everything contrasted strangely with Mahommedan India—the India that I had known best. The people were so thin, so black, so scantily clothed, compared to their Northern countrymen!

From my 'rickshaw, in Madras, I looked with

interest at the public buildings and general street scenes of one of the biggest and most important of Indian cities; and my homesick heart found joy in the sight and smell and sound of the ocean lapping the beach.

At Madura, one of the first things that attracted my attention was the extreme enlargement of the women's ear-lobes. In every case, nothing remained of the original lobe but a thread of skin which, surrounding heavy gold and silver jewels, hung to the shoulder. The lobe of the ear is cut when the child is but three days old, rolls of cotton in gradually increasing sizes being inserted for one year; then leaden rings, one after the other, are added, until the lobes touch the shoulders, usually when the girl is thirteen years of age. The ears are then ready for jewels.

The political and religious life of the South Country Hindu has always found its highest development at Madura; and I had visited the city especially to see the Great Gopura, a typical and magnificent specimen of Dravidian architecture.

I stopped long to view the exterior of the Gopura, where pyramids made up of skilfully carved figures—gods, elephants, horses, lions, peacocks—closely crowded and of gorgeous color, against a background of red and gold, climb higher and higher until lost in a general iridescence against the blinding blue of the Indian sky.

In the Choltry or "Hall of a Thousand Columns," where once the pious Tirumal Naik received at stated intervals the god Siva and did homage to him, noisy merchants displayed their wares of every description, and only with difficulty did I escape their importunities and see with any satisfaction whatever the wonderful carving of the four rows of columns which form the Choltry.

However, the huge dragons and other figures of stone were of less interest to me than the marvelous life by which I was surrounded.

With freshly made caste marks on face and arms and body, solemn Hindus passed me on their way to the quiet corners, where, in the glimmering half light of a smoky lamp, hideous little idols, bedaubed with paint and hung with flower garlands, awaited their devotees.

As I stood bewildered at the clamor of human voices and the multiplicity of carved figures, I heard the sound of jangling bells and glanced up just in time to step from the path of a procession of holy elephants, gaudily painted and caparisoned, carrying the gold bowls of bathing water for the gods. At the same moment the worshipers in the temple crowded forward and, touching with awed fingers the swaying sides of the great beasts, fell prostrate on their faces, lying thus till the procession had passed.

I visited the famed Great Banyan of Madura; and, although not particularly charmed with Dravidian architecture in the tiring confusion of its detail, I drove out to the Teppa Kulam Temple, before the dying sun warned me it was time to seek the shelter of my hotel.

It was an ideal tropical night — blue and dreamy with moonlight—when from the deck of our comfortable steamship I bade farewell to India.

Before me lay the white city of Tuticorin slowly fading into darkness. Farther and farther I gazed until the beyond was pierced by the light of memory which, shining bright through five busy years, illuminated the trodden path and dispelled the few black clouds which still hung low.

Good-by, my India!

Though I may never see again your burning plains, your snow-crowned hills, your sun-kissed children, my heart will always hold you dear, for you have given me the greatest blessing of earth or heaven—peace!